SPIRIT OF
# SURREY

**MIKE COPE**

First published in Great Britain in 2011
Copyright text and photographs © 2011 Mike Cope.

British Library Cataloguing-in-Publication Data
A CIP record for this title is available from the British Library

ISBN 978 0 85710 058 0

**PiXZ Books**
Halsgrove House, Ryelands Business Park,
Bagley Road, Wellington, Somerset TA21 9PZ
Tel: 01823 653777, Fax: 01823 216796
email: sales@halsgrove.com

An imprint of Halstar Ltd, part of the Halsgrove group of companies
Information on all Halsgrove titles is available at: www.halsgrove.com

Printed and bound in China by
Topan Leefung Printing Ltd

# Introduction

A popular misconception of Surrey is that it is better known for its suburbia than its scenery – a busy, affluent and overpopulated shire, whose towns are merely dormitories for the capital. Whilst there is some truth in this assertion, it does ignore the fact that there is a surprising amount of unspoilt countryside and open space. Although Surrey contains more miles of motorway than any other county, it also contains more acres of woodland – a 22.4% coverage compared to the national average of 11.8%. Indeed the image on page 40, 'Sunset over the strawberry fields', was taken just a few steps away from the busy A3 – one of the most important trunk roads in the county. Divided east to west by the North Downs, pierced by the valleys of the Wey and Mole and dotted with hills and open heathland, Surrey has many hidden places to discover and explore. The National Trust owns many of the open spaces and historic houses, and seeks to preserve and protect them for future generations.

Narrow boats on the River Wey Navigation near Papercourt Lock, Send.

*Opposite:* Silent Pool, Albury. The crystal clear waters come from a freshwater spring which has passed through the chalk hillside of the North Downs.

The old parish church of Albury has a mortuary chapel remodelled by the renowned Victorian architect, Augustus Pugin.

*Opposite:*
The Catholic Apostolic church, built by Henry Drummond, owner of Albury Park, in 1840.

The 'Pugin chimneys' are a feature of the Albury village skyline.

*Opposite:*
The Tour Series bike race around Woking Town Centre.

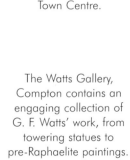

The Watts Gallery, Compton contains an engaging collection of G. F. Watts' work, from towering statues to pre-Raphaelite paintings.

Pair of brightly coloured macaws at Birdworld, Farnham.

*Opposite:* Peacock at Jenny Wren Farm, Birdworld, Farnham.

'Tripping the light fantastic' across The Stepping Stones, Box Hill, Dorking.

*Opposite:* The Zig Zag road up Box Hill, Dorking.

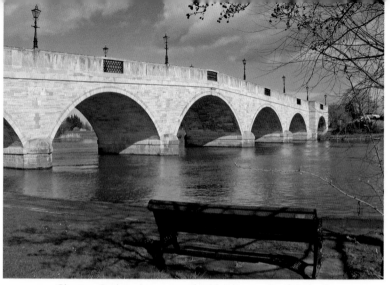

Chertsey Bridge. A seven-arched bridge made of Purbeck
stone and completed in 1784.

*Opposite:* Field of oil seed rape at Chilworth.

The Watts Chapel, Compton. Detail of the stunning gesso interior:
a crimson seraph with hands raised in blessing.

*Opposite:* The hilltop church of St Martha's on the North Downs Way.

St Catherine's chapel, Guildford – reputedly used by medieval pilgrims travelling from Winchester to Canterbury.

The Cathedral of the Holy Spirit, Stag Hill, Guildford.

*Opposite:*
The Sandpits, Horsell Common, where the Martians landed in H.G. Wells' nineteenth century classic *The War of the Worlds*.

*Above:* Hampton Court Palace. Henry VIII's historic red brick Tudor palace, spectacularly illuminated at night.

*Right:* A dramatic winter ice rink on the banks of the River Thames, set against the stunning backdrop of an iconic royal landmark.

The Muslim burial
ground in Maybury.

*Opposite:*
Frensham Little Pond
frozen over.

Steps out of the Devil's Punch Bowl, Hindhead.

*Opposite:* A frosty winter's day near Papercourt Lock, Send.

Winter sunset at Leith Hill.

*Opposite:* Meadow in Old Woking, bathed in evening sunlight.

Detail of railway carriage
at Woking Station.

*Opposite:*
The ruins of Newark Priory,
Ripley – dissolved by
Henry VIII in 1539.

Under the gunnera,
The Valley Gardens,
Virginia Water.

Band of the Irish Guards at the Guards Polo Club, Windsor Great Park.

Opposite: Stunning display of spring azaleas in
The Valley Gardens, Virginia Water.

Birds of prey flying display at Painshill Park, Cobham.

St Barnabus' church,
Ranmore 'Church
of the North Downs'.

Windswept Scots pine on the Pilgrim's Way, Ranmore Common.

Opposite: Close up of *Echinops* in the country garden, RHS Wisley.

Martian sculpture in Woking town centre, commissioned to mark the centenary of H.G. Wells' *The War of the Worlds*.

*Opposite:*
O'Neill's pub, a popular drinking haunt in Woking town centre.

Dorking cemetery, basking in autumn sunshine and not in the least bit gloomy.

South front of Clandon Park, West Clandon.

St Edward the Martyr Orthodox church, Brookwood. A small monastic community was established in 1982 to care for the church in which the sacred relics of an English king are enshrined.

*Opposite:* Sunset over the strawberry fields at Home Farm, Godalming.

Sweet chestnut tree along Chestnut Lane, Chobham.

*Opposite:*
One of the ponds on the edge of Chobham Place Woods.

Autumn leaves at Chobham Place Woods.

Brockham has one of the
largest firework displays
in the United Kingdom.

*Opposite:*
Bonfire and church on
Brockham village green.

The cascade at Virginia Water lake – built by George III in the 1750s.

*Opposite:* A beech tree on the edge of Virginia
Water lake sheds its last remaining leaves.

The Totem Pole near
Virginia Water lake – a
gift from the people
of Canada to HM
Queen Elizabeth II.

*Above:* The towers and turrets of Royal Holloway College, Egham with its flamboyant red stonework and French Renaissance style.

*Below:* Detail of 'The Purgatorial ladder' – a medieval wall painting in Chaldon church.

Bonfire shades of *Liquidambar* (North American sweet gum) at RHS Wisley.

*Opposite:* The clock that overhangs the main road at Abinger
Hammer, portrays the figure of 'Jack the Blacksmith'
who strikes the hour with his hammer.

Gomshall village sign,
depicting mill
and waterwheel.

*Above:* The cenotaph in Woking town centre, with newly remodelled entrance to The Peacocks.

*Below:* The Guildhall and overhanging clock in Guildford High Street.

Winter sunset on Holmbury Hill.

*Opposite:* Snow enfolds the summit of Leith Hill –
the highest point in south-east England.

The Canal and Laboratory, RHS Wisley – seen in a different light – on an evening illumination trail.

*Opposite:*
The front entrance to the Glasshouse, RHS Wisley, festooned with seasonal lights.

A spectacular light display illuminates the Glasshouse at RHS Wisley.

Boardwalk across Thursley Nature Reserve.

*Opposite:*
The toposcope on Holmbury Hill is a popular meeting point for
mountain bikers, and the starting point for numerous trails.

View of Dorking from the North Downs Way.

*Opposite:*
Heathland on the boundary of MOD land, near Lightwater Country Park.

The ruins of Woking Palace, a favourite residence of Henry VIII, during the earlier part of his reign.

St Michael's, Betchworth – used for filming 'Four Weddings and a Funeral'.

*Opposite:* The ruins of Waverley Abbey – the first Cistercian abbey in England, and inspiration for Sir Walter Scott's novel *Waverley*.

Southbound train leaving Woking Station, one summer evening

## WHAT'S IN YOUR GUIDEBOOK?

**Independent authors** Impartial up-to-date information from our travel experts who meticulously source local knowledge.

**Experience** Thomas Cook's 165 years in the travel industry and guidebook publishing enriches every word with expertise you can trust.

**Travel know-how** Contributions by thousands of staff around the globe, each one living and breathing travel.

**Editors** Travel-publishing professionals, pulling everything together to craft a perfect blend of words, pictures, maps and design.

**You, the traveller** We deliver a practical, no-nonsense approach to information, geared to how you really use it.

## ABOUT THE AUTHOR

Jane Anson is a writer and columnist, based in Bordeaux, France – just two hours from Toulouse – and the author Thomas Cook's HotSpot Corsica and CitySpot Bordeaux guidebooks. She also writes widely for the *Telegraph*, the *Irish Independent*, *Food & Travel*, *Gourmet Traveller* and *Wine & Spirit* magazines, plus a number of other international publications.

# CITYSPOTS
# TOULOUSE

Jane Anson

**Written by Jane Anson**

**Published by Thomas Cook Publishing**
A division of Thomas Cook Tour Operations Limited
Company registration No: 1450464 England
The Thomas Cook Business Park, 9 Coningsby Road
Peterborough PE3 8SB, United Kingdom
Email: sales@thomascook.com, Tel: +44 (0)1733 416477
www.thomascookpublishing.com

**Produced by The Content Works Ltd**
Aston Court, Kingsmead Business Park, Frederick Place
High Wycombe, Bucks HP11 1LA
www.thecontentworks.com

Series design based on an original concept by Studio 183 Limited

ISBN: 978-1-84157-889-7

First edition © 2008 Thomas Cook Publishing
Text © Thomas Cook Publishing
Maps © Thomas Cook Publishing/PCGraphics (UK) Limited
Transport map © Communicarta Limited

Series Editor: Kelly Anne Pipes
Production/DTP: Steven Collins

Printed and bound in Spain by GraphyCems

Cover photography (Pont Neuf) © Art Kowalsky/Alamy

# CONTENTS

## SYMBOLS KEY

The following symbols are used throughout this book:

ⓐ address ⓣ telephone ⓕ fax ⓦ website address ⓔ email
ⓛ opening times ⓝ public transport connections

The following symbols are used on the maps:

| | | | |
|---|---|---|---|
| ℹ️ information office | | ▇ points of interest | |
| ✈️ airport | | ◯ city | |
| ➕ hospital | | ◯ large town | |
| 🕓 police station | | ◦ small town | |
| 🚌 bus station | | ═ motorway | |
| 🚃 railway station | | ─ main road | |
| Ⓜ metro | | ─ minor road | |
| ✝ cathedral | | ─ railway | |
| ❶ numbers denote featured cafés & restaurants | | | |

Hotels and restaurants are graded by approximate price as follows:
£ budget price  ££ mid-range price  £££ expensive

▶ *The Capitole, Toulouse's 250-year-old town hall*

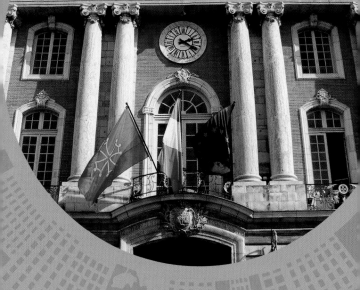

# Introduction

There are some French cities that feel very much part of northern Europe – say Paris, Lille, or Bordeaux – and are all about elegance and sophistication. There are others – Lyon, Marseille, and very definitely Toulouse – that belong to southern Europe and the Mediterranean.

● *Place du Capitole, home to bustling markets and lively bars*

Even the nickname of Toulouse, La Ville Rose, or 'pink city', conjures up images of lazy sunshine and laid back beauty. The name actually comes from the local red clay which the Romans used to build the city, although most of the handsome red brick you can see today dates back to the 15th century.

In terms of economy and size, however, Toulouse is anything but lazy and laid back. Toulouse is the capital of the Midi-Pyrénées, the largest region in metropolitan France. It has 120,000 students, the biggest student population in the country after Paris. And with well over a million inhabitants, the city is the fourth biggest in France.

More importantly, Toulouse is also the fastest growing city in Europe. Aviation and spaceflight have transformed the economy. Almost ten per cent of the population work in the civil aviation and space industries, in particular Airbus and the Space City initiative.

Toulouse's location in the southwest of France, near the Pyrénées mountains and the Spanish border and not far from the Languedoc and the Côte d'Azur, translates into a relaxed, culturally rich lifestyle. The city heaves with late night bars and restaurants, street markets and festivals. As the préfecture (capital) of the Haute-Garonne region it is the unofficial centre of Occitan culture, and many of the festivals revolve around this colourful, passionate and historic community. Toulouse has a good chance of winning the status of European City of Culture in 2013, as a reflection of its lively and rich cultural scene.

# When to go

Toulouse is a top destination at any time of year. In the heat of summer, life moves outdoors, into parks, onto terrace restaurants and bars. You can take boat trips on the Canal du Midi or pop to the coastline for some beach indulgence. In winter, Toulouse's location close to the Pyrénées makes it a great base for adventurous weekend sports. Costs don't vary on- and off-peak as much as in some cities, although in summer it is best to book well in advance.

## SEASONS & CLIMATE
The weather is welcoming most of the year. Spring begins in March or April, with temperatures climbing to around 20°C (68°F). July and August are very hot, with an average temperature of 28°C (82°F) and over ten hours of sunshine per day. Autumn is often rainy, but still warm. Snow has been known in winter, but it is rarely freezing.

## ANNUAL EVENTS
Toulouse is a city that likes to celebrate, and you'll often find yourself in the middle of a festival. The large number of students means that many events are centred on contemporary culture, from film festivals to live music gigs.

### January & February
**Contemporary Dance Festival** Featuring international companies and young artists. ☎ (05) 61 59 98 78 ⓦ www.cdctoulouse.com

**Zoom Arrière** Festival rediscovering forgotten
film classics. 🅐 69 rue du Taur 🅣 (05) 62 30 30 10
🅦 www.lacinemathequedetoulouse.com 🅝 Metro: Capitole

**March & April**

**Flamenco Festival** This feast of Andalusian music
and dancing takes place over ten days in late April.
🅣 (05) 34 25 81 21 🅦 www.festival-flamenco-toulouse.com
**Le Printemps du Rire** Festival of stand-up comedy, theatre and
improvisation. 🅣 (05) 62 21 23 24 🅦 www.printempsdurire.com

🔺 *Aerial view of the city and the Canal du Midi*

## May & June

**Le Marathon des Mots** Free street theatre throughout the city, plus ticketed plays, readings, concerts and dance productions. ☏ (05) 61 99 64 01 ⓦ www.lemarathondesmots.com

**Rio Loco** International world music festival focused on a different country each year. ⓐ Prairie des Filtres rue Laganne ☏ (05) 61 32 77 28 Ⓜ Metro: Esquirol ⓦ www.rio-loco.org

## July & August

**Dance Festival** Contemporary dance events during the first week of July. ☏ (05) 62 30 69 10 ⓦ www.jamescarles.com

**Toulouse In Summer** Over 400 musicians give concerts, often free, at the major parks, galleries and monuments around Toulouse. Expect anything from jazz, rock, tango or hip hop to classical and opera. ☏ (05) 62 27 60 60 ⓦ www.mairie-toulouse.fr

## September & October

**Visual Arts Festival** Also known as Les Printemps de Septembre (Springtime in September), a free festival dedicated to visual arts of all types. ☏ (05) 34 51 39 85 ⓦ www.printempsdeseptembre.com

**Festival de Rue de Ramonville** September street party around Place Jean-Jaurès. ☏ (05) 61 73 00 48 Ⓜ Metro: Jean-Jaurès ⓦ www.festivalramonville-arto.fr

## November & December

**Short Film Festival** Festival of award-winning short films and children's films. ☏ (05) 61 11 02 22 ⓦ www.toulouse-tourisme.com

**Toulouse Antiques Fair** One of France's biggest and best antiques fairs with over 300 dealers descending on the city in November.

Ⓐ Parc des Expositions de Toulouse, Rond point Michel Bénech
Ⓦ www.salon-antiquaires-toulouse.com Ⓛ 10.00–19.00
Ⓜ Metro: Les Arènes. Admission charge
**Marché de Noel** Christmas market with over 130 stands of
presents, decorations and festive food. Ⓐ Place du Capitole
Ⓣ (05) 61 52 74 21 Ⓜ Metro: Capitole

**PUBLIC HOLIDAYS**
**Jour de l'An (New Year's Day)** 1 January
**Lundi de Pâques (Easter Monday)** 24 March 2008,
13 April 2009
**Fête du Travail (Labour Day)** 1 May
**Victoire 1945 (World War II Armistice)** 8 May
**Ascension** 22 May 2008, 11 June 2009
**Lundi de Pentecôte (Whit Monday)** 12 June 2008,
1 June 2009
**Bastille Day/Fête Nationale (French Revolution)** 14 July
**Assomption (Assumption)** 15 August
**Touissant (All Saints Day)** 1 November
**Armistice 1918 (World War I Armistice)** 11 November
**Noël (Christmas Day)** 25 December

On public holidays government departments, banks, shops
and even some restaurants are closed. If a public holiday falls
on a Thursday or a Tuesday, many French like to *faire le pont*
(bridge over) and take a four-day weekend.

# Aeronautical Toulouse

For the past few centuries, Toulouse has been all about flying – both on earth and in space – and today it is one of France's most high tech cities.

Clement Adler, the first human to fly in an aircraft powered by a motor, was born in Muret, 20 km from Toulouse. He worked as an engineer in the city, experimenting at the end of the 19th century with machines that flapped their wings like birds. He eventually managed to get 15 cm (6 in) off the ground in 1886 in a bat-shaped monoplane called *L'École* (the School).

Rather more successfully, Toulouse later became the base of the first regular airline taking off from French soil. Pierre-Georges Latécoère (founder of France's first regular mail and passenger plane in the 1930s), the fighter pilot Jean Daurat, the heroic Jean

Mermoz and the writer and pilot Antoine de Saint-Exupéry all have strong links with the city.

Today, Toulouse is the centre of the European aerospace industry. Alcatel Alenia Space, EADS Astrium, and Galileo have a significant presence in Toulouse, and the headquarters of Airbus SAS has been based here since the 1970s. Almost 12,000 people are employed by Airbus in Toulouse, and you can take tours of its iconic planes, including the new double decker A300. You can also walk onboard the last model of Concorde (see page 94).

In 1997 Toulouse saw the launch of a space-themed adventure park, the Cité de l'Espace (see page 92). Here you can see a recreation of the MIR Space Station, the Sputnik 1 satellite and the Ariane 5 Rocket, as well as watch movies at an IMAX cinema.

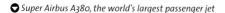

❤ *Super Airbus A380, the world's largest passenger jet*

# History

As with many big cities, Toulouse's location and its wide, navigable river were responsible for its early rise to prominence. The River Garonne was forded in the 8th century BC, and the area became a focal point for trade between the Pyrénées, the Mediterranean and the Atlantic. A large fertile plain north of the city meant that locals could farm and grow food. It was known as *Tolosa*, a name that has remained practically unchanged over the centuries, despite various invasions by the Celts, the Romans and the Visigoths.

The Romans arrived in 125 BC, founding the nearby Narbonne. Toulouse enjoyed a fruitful relationship with them, at first simply as allies. Inevitably, when Julius Caesar arrived and took control of Gaul, Toulouse became part of the Roman Empire. The city moved to its current position, built walls around its border as a symbol of imperial favour, and became one of the most powerful cities in the empire. It was filled with popular baths, aqueducts, circuses, theatres, a forum, and a sophisticated sewage system. The Saint Sernin basilica, today one of Toulouse's most visited and beautiful local attractions, was founded in memory of the city's first Christian bishop, who was martyred on the site.

The Visigoths, who took over the city after the Romans in the 5th century, realised what a treasure they had. Give or take one or two invasions, things ran smoothly and successfully for Toulouse. From the 9th to the 13th centuries, Toulouse was the seat of one of the most beautiful courts of Europe. A refined civilisation and culture developed, giving birth to such things as the literature of the Langue d'Oc, and the *troubadours*, wandering musicians who travelled the country composing and playing their music. The city officially became part of France in 1271.

The Inquisition had a big effect on Toulouse, and for almost 400 years the city was the centre of the Inquisition in southern France. Countless heretics were burned at the stake. The city remained economically successful, thanks to the popularity of its local fabric dye, woad, and many of the large properties and public buildings that dominate the downtown area today were built during this time. In a bright moment, the University was also founded. Toulouse remained relatively independent until the French Revolution in 1789.

Toulouse's luck held out after the Revolution as well, paradoxically in the fact that it missed many of the industrial developments of the 19th century. Unlike so many cities, this means that there are now very few ugly industrial factories in the downtown area, and many historic monuments are still fully intact.

The city has enjoyed strong economic development in recent decades, in part due to the decentralization of many ministries, such as weather, civil aviation, and the *Centre National d'Études Spatiales* (National Space Centre). The future history of Toulouse looks set to rocket.

🔺 *Ready for lift-off!*

# Lifestyle

Southern France is known for its relaxed lifestyle, and Toulouse is no exception. People like to work fewer hours and enjoy themselves more. Their laid back, welcoming attitude extends to visitors. Even at sporting events rivalry is friendly rather than fierce, and you'll often hear Toulouse fans singing the opposing team's songs to keep the atmosphere sweet. The large number of visiting students also contributes to the feel of a thriving, international city. Most weekends you'll find a celebration or festival going on.

Restaurants tend to serve lunch between 12.00 and 14.00, and dinner between 19.00 and 22.00, but you'll find more exceptions to this rule than in many French cities. Most restaurant staff are very relaxed with children, and you will often see families eating together in the evening.

### CANAL DU MIDI

This 240 km World Heritage classified canal stretches from above Toulouse right down to Sète. Originally conceived as a shortcut between the Atlantic and the Mediterranean, it has 103 locks and countless bridges, dams and a tunnel. It snakes around the city of Toulouse. To see it at its best, cross the Jardin Japonais, part of the Jardin Compans Caffarelli (see page 93), stroll along to the Port de l'Embouchure and take a boat trip up to the lock gates. Boat trips are available from NaviCanal (see page 58).

🔺 *Peacefully meandering the Canal du Midi*

As with anywhere in France, it is appreciated if you try to speak a bit of the language. Many people do speak English but it does pay to greet shopkeepers and restaurant owners with a *bonjour* and *s'il vous plaît*.

Throughout its history Toulouse has been a highly religious city, and this is still true today. Largely Catholic, there are numerous religious festivals and active churches all over the city. If you would like to attend a service try the Saint Sernin basilica (see page 60), one of the best examples of a Roman church in the country, or Saint Pierre des Cuisines (see page 66), the oldest religious building in Toulouse. Be aware that, partly as a result of this strong Catholicism in the city, almost everything is closed on Sundays.

# Culture

Toulouse is a young, vibrant, international city. It is filled with students from all over the world, and with high tech international companies employing young and ambitious staff. As a result, the city is heaving with arts and culture all year round, from theatre and music to street art and dance. Visiting groups come regularly, drawn by the 15 large scale festivals throughout the year. Toulouse looks set to win the status of European City of Culture 2013.

## MUSIC

Big name international musicians generally play at the city's main stadium on Ramier Island, in the middle of the Garonne river (see pages 76–87). George Michael, for example, sang here during his 2006 tour. Concerts by local musicians and sporting events also take place at the stadium. Classical music is regularly performed at the **Théâtre du Capitole** (❸ Pl du Capitole ❶ (05) 61 63 13 13 ❿ www.theatre-du-capitole.org), and some of the best concerts you will hear are of classical piano, organ or string music, often beautifully staged among the city's many historical monuments. Smaller theatre workshops and concerts spring up regularly in arts theatres and bars everywhere. There are festivals all year round, adding to the feeling that this is a city embracing its cultural heritage.

● *The Capitole's stunning reception hall, the Salles des Illustres*

## MUSEUMS

The rich cultural life of this southwest city is easily seen by the wide range of excellent museums on offer, many housed in the historical buildings that criss-cross the downtown area. One museum not to miss is Musée des Augustins (see page 68) with paintings and sculpture dating back to the Middle Ages and a wonderful adjoining convent.

## CONTEMPORARY SCENE

It is contemporary art that really makes Toulouse stand out. There is a thriving graffiti scene that has, controversially, become famous across Europe. Look out for sloe-eyed nymph girls in provocative poses, drawn by the notorious Miss Van of the graffiti artist club Hanky Panky Girls. Miss Van now lives in Barcelona and exhibits in galleries across Europe and in New York, but her influence in her hometown of Toulouse is still huge and there are dozens of young graffiti artists hoping to follow in her high-heeled footsteps. Along the quays are dozens of free galleries showcasing the latest works from young artists, while the more established talents make it into Les Abattoirs (see page 81), a contemporary art space that has revitalised an entire section of the Left Bank of the city.

▶ *A heady mix of architectural styles in central Toulouse*

# Shopping

Shopping and food make a good combination in Toulouse. The city is heaving with excellent markets, upmarket delicatessens, bakeries and *épiceries* (grocery stores). Head to the covered Victor Hugo market (see pages 47 and 70) for locally produced *foie gras*, cheeses, charcuteries, and of course the best Toulouse sausage you can buy. There are lots of good food and wine shops around the outside, plus small eateries on the first floor. Don't forget to pop into a *cave à vins* (wine cellar – two of the best are actually stalls within Victor Hugo market) and get some expert advice on the region's local wines.

Shopping and clothes are also well matched here. The large department stores **Galeries Lafayette** (ⓐ 77 rue Alsace Lorraine) and **Nouvelles Galeries** (ⓐ 4–8 rue Lapeyrouse) are handy, but for original designer clothes and shoes concentrate on the chic streets between Place President Wilson, Place St Georges and the Musée des Augustins. There are also a number of quirky vintage clothes shops.

Rue Croix Baragnon and the small streets around the Place St Etienne are the best places to find trendy interior design shops, with anything from lamps to rugs to sculptures.

Books and records are easy to find around Place du Capitole. Besides a number of very well stocked libraries, Toulouse boasts an impressive *médiathèque* (see page 97).

If you're looking for an indoor shopping centre, head for Carrefour at Portet-sur-Garonne (see page 99), or St Georges, near Place St Georges.

## USEFUL SHOPPING PHRASES

**What time do the shops (this shop) open/close?**
A quelle heure ouvrent/ferment les magasins
(ce magasin)?
*Ah kel ur oovra / fairm lay magazahn
(suh magazahn)?*

**How much is this?**
Ça fait combien?
*Sa fay kombyen?*

**Do you take credit cards?**
Prenez-vous les cartes de crédit?
*Pruhnay voo lay kart duh kraydee?*

**My size is...**
Ma taille est...
*Ma tie eh...*

**I'll take this one, thank you**
Je prends celui-ci/celle-ci merci
*Juh prohn selwee-see / sell see mehrsee*

**Can I try this on?**
Puis-je essayer ceci?
*Pwee juh ehssayeh suhsee?*

# Eating & drinking

Toulouse is a city for gourmets. As in much of southwest France, one of the key local specialities is duck. You can gorge yourself on *foie gras*, the controversial fattened duck liver paté that is not for the delicate-hearted, as well as *rillettes* (a coarser duck paté), hearty duck soups and potatoes sautéed in duck fat. Markets have an endless variety of these products and many will offer free samples.

Local cheese is also good. Try *brebis*, sheep's milk cheese from the nearby Pyrénées mountains, often laced with spices or even local liqueurs. Toulouse's river, canal and location between the Atlantic and the Mediterranean mean that many bistros do wonderful seafood platters, with everything from lobster to tiny *boulots* (periwinkles).

The local vineyards add colour and warmth to your meal, and as many are close to the city, it is worth taking a day trip

### PRICE CATEGORIES
Based on the average price per head for a two-course dinner, excluding drinks. Lunch will usually be cheaper, and most restaurants offer a very good value *prix fixe* (set menu) option at lunchtime.
**£** Under €18  **££** €18–€30  **£££** Over €30

● *Pavement cafes, perfect for watching the world go by*

◆ *View through an archway into a courtyard in central Toulouse*

## CASSOULET

Cassoulet is the most famous of Toulouse dishes. It is a rich, slow-cooked bean casserole containing meat (typically pork sausages, mutton or duck), *couennes* (pork skin) and white haricot beans. The dish is named after the cassole, the distinctive oval covered earthenware pot in which cassoulet is traditionally cooked. It is traditional to use the pot from the previous cassoulet in order to give a base for the next one – in theory just having one endless pot on the go. You'll find many restaurants, both in Toulouse and the surrounding areas, that have their own versions of the dish. In the city centre, **La Cave au Cassoulet** (🅐 54 rue Peyrolières 🅣 (05) 56 13 60 30) claims to make the most authentic version.

out to discover some local producers (see pages 116–27). There are a number of good traditional wine merchants, plus two stalls in Victor Hugo market which provide local bottles. The student population also ensures there are plenty of beer joints, cocktail bars and wine bars, many around Place du Capitole and Rue Gambatta.

Local food intermingles with international cuisine and the city has literally thousands of cafés, bars, pizzerias, oriental and other international eateries. The more upmarket restaurants are concentrated around Place President Wilson, and Place du Capitole, while smaller neighbourhood favourites can be found in the narrow streets leading down to the Garonne river around Pont Neuf or in St Cyprien. For something different, try **L'Occitania**, a floating restaurant moored on the Canal du Midi (❸ L'Ecluse Bayard ❶ (05) 61 63 06 06).

Restaurant bills are almost always *service compris* (service included), so tipping or rounding up is an extra to acknowledge good service. Major credit cards are accepted pretty much everywhere, although you might need cash for the smaller fast-food joints and kebab shops.

As of January 2008, smoking is banned in all public spaces, including restaurants and bars.

### USEFUL DINING PHRASES

**I would like a table for ... people**
Je voudrais une table pour ... personnes
*Juh voodray oon tabl poor ... pehrson*

**Waiter/waitress**
Monsieur/mademoiselle (the traditional term
*garçon* is no longer considered polite)
*M'syer/madmwahzel*

**May I have the bill please?**
L'addition, s'il vous plaît
*L'adission, sill voo play*

**Could I have this rare/medium/well cooked**
Je le voudrais saignant/à point/bien cuit
*Juh luh voodray saynyohn/ah pwan/bi-yen kwee*

**I am vegetarian**
Je suis végétarien/végétarienne
*Juh swee vehjaytaryan/vehjaytaryen*

**Where are the toilets please?**
Où sont les toilettes s'il vous plaît?
*Oo son lay twahlet, sill voo play?*

**Can I see the wine list?**
La carte des vins s'il vous plaît
*Lah cart day vahn sill voo play*

🔺 *Du pain, s'il vous plaît*

# Entertainment & nightlife

Toulouse's nightlife is lively, constantly changing and evolving. You'll find plenty to do just by wandering around and stumbling on bars, theatres and clubs, particularly around the Place du Capitole. If you like to plan, local listings magazines include the free *Toulouse Cultures*, *Les Clés de L'Art* and the good value *Toulouse Flashebdo*. These are available from the tourist office, magazine stands and some hotels.

There are five main theatres in the city as well as countless smaller establishments. Try the traditional Théâtre Garonne (see page 84) or the more avant-garde **Nouveau Théâtre Jules-Julien** (ⓐ 6 avenue des Écoles Jules-Julien ⓣ (05) 61 25 79 92). For classical music, head to the Théâtre du Capitole (see page 20). The Halle aux Grains (see pages 96–7) has a mix of classical and modern music, plus contemporary dance. The **Église St Pierre des Chartreux** (ⓐ 21 rue Valade ⓣ (05) 61 21 99 34) is a picturesque scene for concerts staged throughout the year, from organ recitals to local choirs. The music scene gets distinctly hipper at newer spaces such as **Vente du Sud** (ⓐ 170 avenue de Lespinet ⓣ (05) 62 73 44 77), where alternative musicians congregate.

There are bars everywhere around Place du Capitole, Place Saint Georges, Place President Wilson and Rue de Metz. For an edgier feel, head for emerging areas such as the far side of Pont Neuf, around Rue de la République, or the roads around the Grand Rond. The multi-use stadium (see page 36) often

ⓞ *Place du Capitole by night*

◆ *Dinner aboard a quayside péniche*

welcomes big international names and many bars and restaurants have live music.

Expect the drinking and dancing to go on until late, with most places staying open until 02.00 or 03.00. Good bars include Le Zénith and Chapeau Rouge (see page 87). For clubbers, there are frequent DJ nights at Parc Expo (see page 87). A new concept at Le Havana (see page 102) is Toulouse Indie Night, where an English band and a local Toulouse band both play a set.

In summer, even when the bars have closed up for the night, life moves out onto the streets. Around the Pont Neuf bridge and other open spaces, you can join late night revellers chatting, dancing, or cramming into the few small clubs and bars that remain open until dawn.

And if you're over 21 and looking to burn some cash, there's also a large casino, the Salies-du-Salat (see page 102), with over 120 slot machines, four roulette tables, a restaurant and a piano bar.

Film fanatics have plenty of options, and many of the local cinemas screen English language films. *Version originale* (VO) means a screening in the original language, with sublitles. Around Place du Capitole, you'll find **Cinémathèque Toulouse** (ⓐ 69 rue du Taur ⓦ www.lacinemathequedetoulouse.com), **ABC** (ⓐ 13 rue Saint-Bernard ⓦ www.abc-toulouse.net) and **Utopia Toulouse** (ⓐ 24 rue Montardy ⓦ www.cinemas-utopia.org/toulouse). You could also try **Cratère Toulouse** (ⓐ 95 grand rue Saint-Michel ⓦ www.cinemalecratere.com) or **Mega CGR** (ⓐ Centre Commercial Leclerc Blagnac ⓦ www.cgrcinemas.fr). For arty cinema, make the trek to **Ramonville** (ⓐ l'Autan ⓣ (05) 61 73 89 03) and Auzielle (ⓐ Studio 7 ⓣ (05) 61 39 02 37).

# Sport & relaxation

Toulouse is a healthy city of green spaces, clear rivers and great footpaths. Rugby is by far the biggest spectator sport, and locals are fiercely proud of their team winning the European championship in 1996, 2003 and 2005.

## SPECTATOR SPORTS

**Stade Municipal de Toulouse** Nicknamed *Le TéFéCé*, or *Les Violets* for their purple shirts, the local football team Toulouse FC is becoming increasingly successful. The stadium has a capacity of over 35,000 and was one of the key stages in the 1998 World Cup. ⓐ 1 allée Gabriel Biénès, Île du Ramier ⓣ 0892 700 831 ⓦ www.tfc.info ⓝ Bus: 12, 52

**Stade Toulousain** The biggest rugby matches are played at the Stade Municipal de Toulouse (see above), although the team's home stadium has recently been renovated and can hold almost 20,000 spectators. ⓐ Stade Ernest Wallen, 114 Rue Troènes ⓣ 08 92 69 31 15 ⓦ www.stadetoulousain.fr ⓝ Metro: Arènes

## PARTICIPATION

**L'Aeroclub Air France de Toulouse** Established aeronautical club. ⓐ 4 Avenue Jean-René Lagasse, Balma ⓣ (05) 61 34 85 11 ⓦ www.acaf-toulouse.com

**Bicycle hire** Movimento offer bicycle hire with outlets at the Square du Général Charles de Gaulle, the bus station, and Port Saint-Sauveur. ⓐ 5 Port Saint-Sauveur ⓣ (05) 34 30 03 00 ⓛ 10.30–13.00, 14.00–18.40 Mon–Sat ⓝ Bus: 22 to Port St Etienne

**Elastic Jump** Most bungee jumping takes place near Castres, about 90 minutes away. ⓐ 1 chemin de Castillon, Pechbonnieu ① (05) 61 74 64 00 ⓦ www.elasticjump.com

**Swimming** Complex of indoor and outdoor swimming pools on Ramier Island. The real discovery is the Parc des Sports Summer Pool, with its rockeries and 1950s architecture. ⓐ allée Gabriel-Biénès ① (05) 61 22 31 35 ① Indoor pool: 09.00–19.00 (school holidays); 16.00–19.00 Mon–Fri, 10.00–12.30, 15.00–19.00 Sat & Sun (rest of year); Outdoor pool: 09.00–20.00, late June–Aug; 09.00–19.00, Sept; closed rest of year; times vary so always phone ahead ⓝ Bus: 12

## RELAXATION

**Yoga School Toulouse** Introductory hours available. ⓐ 46 rue de Metz ① (05) 61 25 17 69 ⓦ www.yogaetmeditation.fr ① Call ahead for class times ⓝ Metro: Capitole

🔺 La Garonne, for leisurely strolling, sightseeing and boating

# Accommodation

It is easy to find good value basic accommodation in Toulouse, but less easy to find luxury. There are just three 4-star hotels, none of which really compete with their equivalent in Paris or London. There are a number of good small hotels and hostels, however, and several apartments to rent.

   Check-in and check-out times are usually fairly relaxed. Breakfast is often extra, and can be expensive, so you might want to skip it and head to one of the many coffee shops around the city. Some hotel rates vary during the busy summer months, but largely speaking prices don't fluctuate too much in high season.

**Toulouse accommodation online** Ⓦ www.toulouse-tourisme.com/hebergement
**Hotel bookings and availability hotline** ☎ 08 92 70 02 97

### HOTELS
**Hôtel Anatole France £** Simple hotel near Place du Capitole, with parking spaces. ⓐ 46 place Anatole France ☎ (05) 61 23 19 96 ⓕ (05) 61 21 47 66 Ⓜ Metro: Capitole

---

**PRICE CATEGORIES**
Based on the average price for a double room for one night.
**£** Under €35   **££** €35–70   **£££** Over €70

**Hôtel des Arts ££** Just off Place Saint Georges, making this small hotel a very handy choice for bars and restaurants. It is pretty basic though, with shared bathrooms for most rooms. ⓐ 1 bis rue Cantegril ⓣ (05) 61 23 36 21 ⓕ (05) 61 12 22 37 ⓝ Metro: Esquirol

**Hôtel Heliot ££** Recently renovated hotel, close to Place President Wilson. Free wireless internet access. ⓐ 3 rue Heliot ⓣ (05) 34 41 39 41 ⓕ (05) 34 41 39 40 ⓦ www.hotel-heliot.com ⓔ reservation@hotel-heliot.com ⓝ Metro: Jean-Jaurès

**Hôtel Jean Mermoz ££** A lovely garden and wide terrace give this hotel an extra cachet. ⓐ 50 rue Matabiau ⓣ (05) 61 63 04 04 ⓦ www.hotel-mermoz.com ⓔ reservation@hotel-mermoz.com ⓝ Metro: Jean-Jaurès

**Hôtel Saint Sernin ££** No prizes for guessing the location of this hotel. Ask for a room with a view of the basilica. ⓐ 2 rue Saint Bernard ⓣ (05) 61 21 73 08 ⓕ (05) 61 22 49 61 ⓦ www.hotel-saint-sernin.new.fr ⓝ Metro: Capitole

**Hôtel de Taur ££** Well placed high above the Place du Capitole, with all bedrooms overlooking a quiet central courtyard. ⓐ 2 rue du Taur ⓣ (05) 61 21 17 54 ⓦ www.hotel-du-taur.com ⓔ contact@hotel-du-taur.com ⓝ Metro: Capitole

**Hôtel des Beaux Arts ££–£££** A fantastic small hotel, perfectly located by Pont Neuf, with many rooms offering views of the river. The rooms are small but well decorated. An excellent bistro is attached, where hotel guests receive a free glass of champagne. ⓐ 1 place du Pont Neuf ⓣ (05) 34 45 42 42 ⓦ www.hoteldesbeauxarts.com ⓔ contact@hoteldesbeauxarts.com ⓝ Metro: Esquirol

**Crowne Plaza £££** Comfortable and well located, if corporate-feeling. Wireless internet and good sized beds and bathrooms. The gym and sauna area has seen better days. ⓐ 7 place du Capitole ⓣ (05) 61 61 19 13 ⓦ www.crowne-plaza-toulouse.com ⓔ hicptoulouse@alliance-hospitality.com ⓝ Metro: Capitole

**Grand Hôtel de l'Opéra £££** The grande dame of Toulouse hotels, with the best location. Slightly stuffy, but very comfortable and good facilities. ⓐ 1 place du Capitole ⓣ (05) 61 21 82 66 ⓔ hotelopera@guichard.fr ⓝ Metro: Capitole

**Hôtel Garonne £££** Probably the smartest boutique hotel in town, this has a Japanese feel, lovely dark woods in the bedrooms and communal areas, and one of the city's best restaurants, called simply '19', directly opposite. Internet in all rooms. ⓐ 22 descente de la Halle aux Poissons ⓣ (05) 34 31 94 80 ⓦ www.hotelgaronne.com ⓔ contact@hotelgaronne.com ⓝ Metro: Esquirol

### APARTMENTS
**Résidence les Princes £** Short-stay apartments for rent in a pretty red-bricked building, not far from La Halle aux Grains with its many concerts. Book well in advance, as there

aren't many available. ⓐ 6 rue des Princes ⓣ (05) 61 80 79 38
ⓦ www.residencelesprinces.com ⓔ infos@residencelesprinces.com
ⓝ Bus: 16, 22

## HOSTELS & CAMPSITES

**Camping de Rupé £** About seven kilometres out of the town
centre, a very popular campsite that can get very lively over the
summer months. ⓐ 21 chemin du Pont-de-Rupé ⓣ (05) 61 70 07 35
ⓝ Bus: 59 from Place Jeanne d'Arc

**Résidence Jolimont £** A fairly large hostel, with beds for up to
100 people. Most rooms have two beds. ⓐ 2 Av Yves Brunaud
ⓣ (05) 34 30 42 80 ⓔ foyerjolimont@wanadoo.fr
ⓝ Metro: Jolimont

● *Pont Neuf, Toulouse's oldest bridge*

# THE BEST OF TOULOUSE

Toulouse is a fairly compact city, so it is easy and fun to visit the key sites, even on a flying visit.

**TOP 10 ATTRACTIONS**

- **Eat cassoulet** Try the most famous local dish, ideally made with Toulouse sausage (see page 29)

- **The weir over the Garonne** Best viewed from the walkway behind Les Abattoirs Museum of Modern Art (see page 81)

- **Culture fix** Toulouse is packed full of art galleries, historical buildings and fabulous churches. Don't miss the Musée des Augustins (see page 68) and the Saint Sernin basilica (see page 60)

- **Victor Hugo market** A great place to spend a few hours. Lots of good food and wine shops around the outside, as well as a host of fascinating market stands (see page 47)

- **Canal du Midi** Rent a barge and cruise down the canal (see page 18)

- **Pont Neuf** Cross over and visit the Château d'Eau photography gallery. (see page 83)

- **Jardin des Plantes** The Botanical Gardens are a great spot to hang out, and perfect for children to enjoy horse rides around the park (see page 65)

- **Ariège Valley** Heading further out towards the Pyrénées, this unspoilt region is great for adventure sports (see page 111)

- **Chic shopping** Concentrate on the trendy streets that run between Place President Wilson, Place St Georges and the Musée des Augustins (see page 24)

- **Cité de l'Espace** Discover the high tech side of the city at this space-themed amusement park (see page 92)

*Much of Toulouse is prettily illuminated at night*

# Suggested itineraries

**HALF-DAY: TOULOUSE IN A HURRY**
Cram a feast of architecture, history and art into a few hours at one of Toulouse's most fabulous art galleries, the Musée des Augustins (see page 68). Then wander down to Place President Wilson and tackle a traditional cassoulet.

**1 DAY: TIME TO SEE A LITTLE MORE**
Grab a more contemporary art fix at Les Abattoirs (see page 81) or the Château d'Eau photography gallery (see page 83) on the far side of the Pont Neuf, Toulouse's oldest bridge. Lunch at the classic Jardins de l'Opéra (see page 74). Pick up a bargain from around Place St Georges, then finish with a walk along the Garonne river and dinner at the Brasserie Les Beaux-Arts (see page 74).

**2–3 DAYS: TIME TO SEE MUCH MORE**
As well as the must-see traditional art, visit trendier galleries such as the Halle aux Poissons (see page 66). It's worth the trek to the Cité de l'Espace (see page 92) or the Airbus site (see page 94) for some high tech wonder. You can relax by the Garonne river and at the Jardin des Plantes (see page 65).

**LONGER: ENJOYING TOULOUSE TO THE FULL**
Toulouse's surrounding towns and villages are packed with possibilities. If you have time, visit Albi (see pages 118–19) and Gaillac (see pages 123–4) or, depending on the season, go skiing or hiking in the mountains (see page 110).

○ *Inside Les Jacobins, one of the city's most striking interiors*

# Something for nothing

You don't need wads of cash to see the best of Toulouse. The city has a thousand hectares of green space – 160 parks, gardens and ancient brick-walled cloisters open free to the public. Add the footpaths along the Canal du Midi and the Garonne River and you can spend your whole holiday walking, wandering and

⬥ *Smart townhouses overlooking the Quai de Tournis*

wondering. The Botanical Gardens (see page 65) are especially good for children, with pony rides and grass track biking, although there is a charge for these.

The Chaussée de Bazacle gives the best free view of Toulouse, with water cascading over a weir at one of the widest points of the river. Or head to the other side of the river for EDF Bazacle (see page 64), an exhibition space in a hydroelectric power station where photographers regularly display their talent.

Art is open to all in Toulouse. Visit photo galleries such as Galerie de la Halle aux Poissons (see page 66) for free, and don't ignore the fabulous street art graffiti around the city. Increasingly, it is the underground that has been attracting some of the most exciting artists, with many metro stations exhibiting contemporary sculptures and paintings. Even the art galleries that charge admission are free on the first Sunday of every month.

The Visual Arts Festival in October is one of the city's biggest free celebrations, dedicated to new artistic forms from computer animation to moving sculptures.

The best day to be in town is Sunday, when the city centre is closed to cars and there are small street markets and free entertainment. Pick up a bargain at the Sunday morning flea market around the St Sernin basilica (see page 60) or buy a picnic from the St Aubin farmers' market.

The bustling fruit and vegetable markets Marché Victor Hugo and the Marché des Carmes (see page 70), are on every morning Tues–Sun, along with the biggest (and best value) market on the Boulevard de Strasbourg (see page 100).

# When it rains

In the height of Toulouse's hot summer, you'll be surprised and grateful if you get any rain. If you get a wet day the rest of the year, you won't go wrong if you take shelter in one of the city's many fantastic galleries and museums. Be aware, though, that many of them are closed on Mondays.

If it looks like the weather is setting in, head for the Cité de L'Espace (see page 92) or the Airbus site (see page 94), which is the largest aeronautical plant in Europe. The guided tours and sights, including the huge Airbus assembly hall and the first production model of Concorde, will keep adults and children amused all day.

Toulouse's many cinemas will help you stay dry in the evening. Try the Cinémathèque (see pages page 35 & 65–6) or one of the bigger multiscreen complexes in a commercial centre on the outskirts of the city. They often show English-language films in the original – check for VO, which stands for *version originale*.

When it is sunny, a great thing to do is walk round Toulouse's 50 or so *hôtel particuliers* – smart merchants' houses that date back mainly to the 15th and 16th centuries – to admire the carved exteriors. When it is raining, it's even better to head to one of these buildings that are open to visitors, such as the Hotel d'Assézat (see page 65), which houses the Fondation Bemberg. Not only does this contain a fascinating art collection, but also hosts regular events for getting children interested in art and history.

And don't forget that a spot of rain makes the perfect excuse to settle down for some serious eating. Take your pick from some of the finest restaurants in France, warm your heart and body

◆ *The 14th-century cloister within the Musee des Augustins*

with a hearty cassoulet or other Toulouse sausage speciality, or head to the small food stands on the first floor of the Victor Hugo market to choose between dozens of good value, fresh foods.

# On arrival

## TIME DIFFERENCE

Toulouse is on European Standard Time (GMT plus one hour).
Daylight saving applies, with clocks going forward one hour in
spring and back one hour in autumn on the same date as the UK.

## ARRIVING
### By air
**Toulouse-Blagnac Airport** (ⓣ (05) 61 42 44 00
ⓦ www.toulouse.aeroport.fr) is 8 km northwest of the centre.

The Navette Aéroport Bus (ⓣ (05) 34 60 64 00) connects to
the central railway station, leaving every 20 minutes between
07.35–00.15 and returning between 05.00–20.20.

Taxis (ⓣ (05) 61 30 02 54) are on the Arrivals level by door C.
Fares are around 22 euros for one person without luggage.
The journey can take anything from 15 minutes to an hour,
depending on traffic.

### By rail
The main railway station is Gare Matabiau (ⓐ Blvd Pierre Semard
ⓣ (05) 61 10 10 00). A metro station, Marengo, is directly underneath.
**SNCF Train Ticket Office** ⓐ 5 rue Peyras ⓣ (08) 92 35 35 35
ⓦ www.sncf.fr ⓒ 09.30–18.30 Mon–Sat

### By road
The central bus station, Gare Routière (ⓐ Blvd Pierre Semard
ⓣ (05) 61 61 67 67 ⓒ 08.00–19.00) is right by the main railway

station. A number of bus companies serve the surrounding areas. Try Eurolines (☎ (05) 61 26 40 04) or Intercars (☎ (05) 61 58 14 53).

Traffic can be very heavy during rush hour. There are several new car parks in the centre, including at Victor Hugo, Capitole and Esquirol. For information visit ⓦ www.vincipark.com.

## By water
The Canal du Midi runs right through the city centre, and you can cruise all the way to Toulouse from either Bordeaux or Marseille.

### IF YOU GET LOST, TRY …

**Sorry to bother you, but…**
Excusez moi de vous déranger, mais…
*Ekskoozay mwah duh voo dayronjay, may…*

**Could you tell me the way to…**
Comment fait-on pour aller a …
*Kohmohn feyt-ohn poor al-lay ah …*

**Do you speak English?**
Parlez-vous anglais?
*Parlay vu ohnglay?*

**Could you point to it on my map?**
Pouvez-vous me le montrer sur la carte?
*Poo vay voo muh luh montray soor la kart?*

**Toulouse**

0 _____ 200 metres
0 _____ 200 yards

A624

Bassin de l'Embouchure

Canal du Midi

BOULEVARD DE L'EMBOUCHURE

BOULEVARD DE LA MARQUETTE

RUE DU BERNAIS

COMPANS

RUE HILAIRE CHANDONNET

DE CASSELARDIT

AVENUE

PONT DE L'EMBOUCHURE

PORT DE L'EMBOUCHURE

ALLEE DE BARCELONE

ALLEE DE BRIENNE

Canal de Brienne

RUE DES AMIDONNIERS

LES AMIDONNIERS

Le Mandala

RUE DES AMIDONNIERS

AVE DU GROUPE MORANCE

Ramier du Bazacle

La Garonne

AVE P SEJOURNE

✈ Toulouse Blagnac

BOULEVARD RICHARD WAGNER

Bazacle

RUE MILHES

BOULEVARD RICHARD WAGNER

PONT DES CATALANS

Les Abattoirs

RUE DES FONTAINES

RUE DES BRAIS

BOULEVARD JEAN BRUNHES

AVE DU CHATEAU D'EAU

AVENUE

VOIRE DU TODEC

AVE DE GRANDE BRETAGNE

RUE DES FONTAINES

N

RUE RAYMOND BADIOU

RUE ADOLPHE COLL

RUE VALLIERE

Le Zenith

Ⓜ Patte d'oie

N124

CEPIERE-POLYGONE

RUE ROQUEMAUREL

KOENIGS

AVE DE LOMBEZ

AVE ETIENNE BILLIERS

✚

AVE DE LOMBEZ

GABRIEL

RUE DE LA GRAFFE

SAINT-CYPRIEN

AVE DE LARDENNE

RUE DE NEGOGOUSSES

RUE DU 11 NOVEMBRE 181

🅿Ⓜ Arènes

BOULEVARD

ALLEE MAURICE SARRAUT D25

RUE DE CUGNAUX

RUE CORNEILLE

Hippodrome de la Cepière

ROUTE DE SAINT-SIMON

RUE HENRI DESBALS

RUE

RUE DES ARCS SANS CYPRIEN

R A VALATS

BOULEVARD DEODAT DE SERVERAC

VESTREPAIN

Lycée Déodat de Séverac

Institut Universitaire de Formation des Maîtres

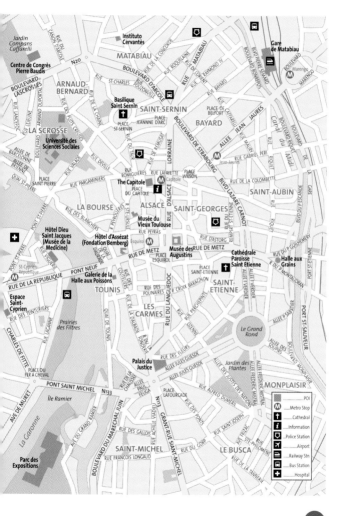

## FINDING YOUR FEET

If you are in Toulouse for a few days, it is worth buying a city pass, *Toulouse en Liberté*, which offers discounts on over 150 attractions around the city.

## ORIENTATION

Keep the Garonne river as your main navigation point, along with the Place du Capitole. In the old part of town, most sights are within the ring of the Boulevards, in a rough square from the Botanical Gardens up to Place de Belfort in the northeast, over to the University in the northwest and then down to Place du Fer à Cheval and the Pont Saint Michel in the southwest. The Ministry of Culture offers tours of its sights and attractions. All visits last around two hours and are held daily in summer, less frequently the rest of the year. For more information contact **Arthemis** ⓐ 6 rue Lt-Colonel Pélissier ⓣ (05) 61 12 13 14 ⓦ www.toulousevisites.com

## GETTING AROUND

Toulouse has an efficient, good value public transport system, though it's compact enough to explore on foot.

### Metro, tram & train

The Toulouse metro system runs from 05.00 to around midnight, or 01.00 on Friday and Saturday nights.
**Line A** covers 15 stations from Balma-Gramont to Basso Cambo.
**Line B**, due for completion in 2009, will run from Ramonville-Saint-Agne to Borderouge, interchanging with Line A at Jean-Jaurés.
**Line C** is a classic railway line with SNCF trains covering eastern Toulouse. It connects to line A at Arènes.

**Line D** runs to the city of Muret.

**Line E**, a tramway planned for completion in 2009, will go from the northwest of the city and Blagnac to Les Arènes metro station, crossing line B at the SNCF Saint Agne station.

## Bus

The local **Tisséo** bus service (☎ (05) 62 11 27 62 🌐 www.tisseo.fr) runs during the day until around 20.00. There are six night buses (N1–N6) leaving from the railway station until just after midnight. La Navette is a small electric bus. Its city centre route is indicated by a dark red line on the pavement. You can hail it from anywhere along the route. Bus tickets can be bought at *tabacs* (tobacconists), news stands, bus, tram and railway stations.

⬇ *Tree-lined avenues make the city a joy to discover on foot*

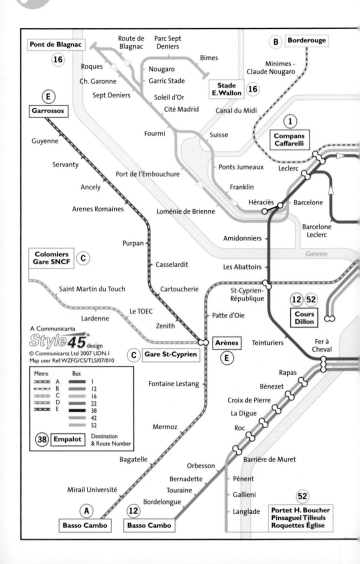

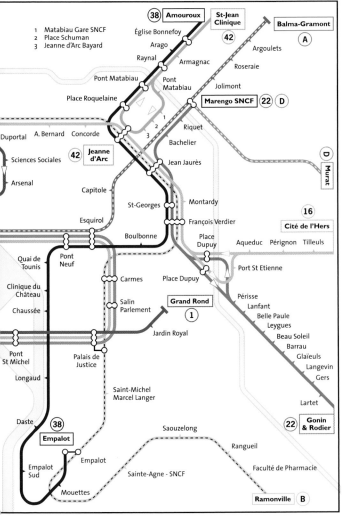

1 Matabiau Gare SNCF
2 Place Schuman
3 Jeanne d'Arc Bayard

38 Amouroux
St-Jean Clinique 42
Balma-Gramont A

Église Bonnefoy
Arago
Raynal
Armagnac
Argoulets
Roseraie

Pont Matabiau
Pont Matabiau
Jolimont
Place Roquelaine
Marengo SNCF 22 D

Duportal A. Bernard Concorde
Riquet
Bachelier
D Murat

Sciences Sociales
42 Jeanne d'Arc
Jean Jaurès

Arsenal
Capitole
St-Georges
Montardy
Esquirol
François Verdier
16
Cité de l'Hers

Boulbonne
Place Dupuy
Aqueduc Pérignon Tilleuls

Quai de Tounis
Pont Neuf
Carmes
Place Dupuy
Port St Etienne

Clinique du Château
Salin Parlement
Grand Rond
Périsse
Lanfant

Chaussée
Jardin Royal
1
Belle Paule
Leygues

Beau Soleil
Barrau

Pont St Michel
Palais de Justice
Glaïeuls
Langevin
Gers

Longaud
Saint-Michel Marcel Langer
Lartet

Daste
38
Gonin & Rodier 22

Empalot
Saouzelong
Rangueil

Empalot Sud
Empalot
Faculté de Pharmacie

Mouettes
Sainte-Agne - SNCF
Ramonville B

### Taxis

There are 24-hour taxi stands at the railway station, at Place
Wilson and at Place Esquirol. It is rather difficult to hail taxis
in the street. There are also 'tourist taxis', in which drivers
guide you around the main sites for around 40 euros an hour.
All taxis are more expensive at night and charge extra for
carrying luggage. Try **Capitole Taxi** (🕐 (05) 34 25 02 50) or
**Radio Taxi Toulousains** (🕐 (05) 61 42 38 38).

### Boat

**Le Capitole** is a tourist boat that sails along the Garonne
river and passes historical monuments and the Île Ramier.
There are night sails in summer. 🅰 Quai de la Daurade
🕐 (05) 61 11 02 33 🕐 Mon–Sun, July–Aug; Tues–Sun, Apr–June
& Oct 🅦 www.toulouse-croisieres.com 🅜 Metro: Esquirol.

For short trips on either the Garonne or Canal du Midi, try **Navi
Canal** (🅰 139 Rue Bonnat 🕐 (05) 61 55 10 91 🅦 www.navicanal.com),
**Baladine** (🅰 62 Port Saint Sauveur 🕐 (05) 61 80 22 26 🕐 Daily
Apr–Nov 🅝 Bus: 22 to Port St Etienne) or **Toulouse Croisieres**
(🅰 7 Port St Sauveur 🕐 (05) 61 25 72 57 🅦 www.toulouse-
croisieres.com 🅜 Bus: 22 to Port St Etienne).

### Car Hire

All major car hire firms have offices in Toulouse, mainly based
at the airport and railway station. Try **Budget** (🅰 49 rue Bayard
🕐 (05) 61 63 18 18 🅦 www.budget.com) or **Europcar** (🕐 Station:
(05) 62 73 41 64; Airport: (08) 25 825 514 🅦 www.europcar.com).

---

▶ *Hôtel-Dieu St-Jacques by the Garonne river*

# The Old Town

The historic centre of Toulouse is on the Right Bank of the Garonne river, and stretches from the Grand Rond and the Palais du Justice up to the Basilique Saint Sernin. It is an attractive maze of mainly pedestrian streets packed with historic buildings and modern bars, shops and restaurants.

A good source of information on many of the monuments, churches, and events listed below is the town hall website ⓦ www.mairie-toulouse.fr.

## SIGHTS & ATTRACTIONS

### Basilique Saint Sernin

This Romanesque basilica, dating back to 1096, is one of Toulouse's most famous and most beautiful sights. Its outstanding feature is the Porte Miégeville, which opens onto the south aisle and is decorated with 12th century sculptures. Concerts are often held here. ⓐ Place Saint Sernin ⓣ (05) 61 21 80 45 ⓦ http://pmaude.free.fr/sernin ⓛ 08.30–11.30, 14.00–17.30 ⓝ Metro: Capitole

### The Capitole

Toulouse's 250 year old town hall, completed in 1759, stands proudly in the centre of the city. On the outside, eight red marble columns represent the eight 'Capitouls' of the municipality. Inside, there are frescoes and various monuments to illustrious past residents of the city. The square outside is the centre of markets and street entertainment throughout the year, and

◆ *The Romanesque basilica of Saint Sernin*

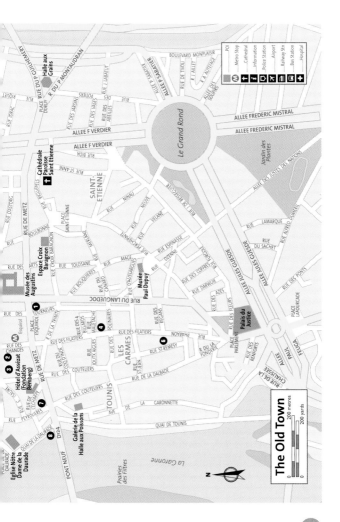

The Old Town

| | POI |
| 🚇 | Metro Stop |
| ✝ | Cathedral |
| ℹ | Information |
| 🛡 | Police Station |
| ✈ | Airport |
| 🚊 | Railway Stn |
| 🚌 | Bus Station |
| ✚ | Hospital |

Le Grand Rond

Jardin des Plantes

Palais du Justice

Halle aux Grains

Cathédrale Paroisse Saint Etienne

SAINT-ETIENNE

Espace Croix Baragnon

Musée des Augustins

Musée Paul Dupuy

LES CARMES

Hôtel d'Assézat (Fondation Bemberg)

TOUNIS

Galerie de la Halle aux Poissons

Église Nôtre Dame de la Daurade

La Garonne

Prairies des Filtres

N

0   200 metres
0   200 yards

is also surrounded by lively cafés and bars. ⓐ Place du Capitole
Ⓝ Metro: Capitole

### Cathédrale Paroisse Saint Etienne

A brooding, immense structure that is a mix of different
architectural styles, having been constructed at various times
over five centuries. There are 17 chapels in here. ⓐ Place Saint
Etienne ⓣ (05) 61 51 03 82 Ⓦ http://cathedrale.toulouse.free.fr
🕒 08.00–19.00 Mon–Sat, 9.00–19.00 Sun Ⓝ Metro: Esquirol

### Chapelle des Carmélites

In the depths of the 12th century Carmélites Convent is this
beautiful small chapel, known as Toulouse's Sistine Chapel.
Concerts are frequently held here. ⓐ 1 Rue du Périgord
ⓣ (05) 61 21 27 60 Ⓦ http://carmelites.monuments-nationaux.fr
🕒 09.30–13.00, 14.00–18.00 Tues–Sun (summer); 10.00–13.00,
14.00–17.30 (winter) Ⓝ Metro: Capitole. Admission charge

### EDF Bazacle

A strange mix of working power station and art gallery – don't
think about it too much, just enjoy one of the best views of the
Garonne river in the city. ⓐ 11 quai Saint Pierre ⓣ (05) 62 30 16 00
🕒 14.00–19.00 Tues–Fri or Tues–Sun during exhibitions;
closed Aug Ⓝ Metro: Compans Caffarelli, then 10 min walk

### Église Nôtre Dame de la Daurade

There are three Nôtre Dame churches in Toulouse – de la Dourade,
de la Taur and de la Dalbade. This one is particularly attractive
because it leads directly out onto the banks of the river. ⓐ 1 place

de la Daurade ☎ (05) 61 21 38 32 Ⓦ www.toulouse-tourisme.com
🕐 08.30–19.00 (summer); 08.30–18.30 (winter) Ⓜ Metro: Esquirol

### Le Grand Rond & Le Jardin des Plantes (Botanical Garden)

Created during the French Revolution, this is the oldest public park
in Toulouse, and over 100 different types of trees and conifers
are found here. At weekends, the park gets very busy, full of
families making use of the many activities, from pony trekking
to roundabouts. ⓐ allées Frederic Mistral 🕐 07.45–dusk

### Hôtel d'Assézat (Fondation Bemberg)

Very attractive former merchant's house. Its previous owner,
Pierre d'Assézat, made his money in the pastel trade. Stroll into
its inner courtyard to view one of the city's most well preserved
16th century facades, or visit the private art collection inside,
with many examples from the Renaissance. ⓐ Place d'Assézat
☎ (05) 61 12 06 89 Ⓦ www.fondation-bemberg.fr 🕐 10.00–12.30,
13.30–18.00 Tues–Sun, open until 21.00 Thur Ⓜ Metro: Esquirol

### Place de la Daurade

A beach in the middle of the city, right on the banks of the
Garonne by the Pont Neuf bridge. Great fun during the summer.
Ⓜ Metro: Esquirol, then 10 min walk

## CULTURE

### Cinémathèque

The kind of arts cinema and exhibition space that every big city
should have. Quirky film festivals held throughout the year. Great

for English-language films, and a good café. ⓐ 69 rue du Taur
ⓣ (05) 62 30 30 10 ⓦ www.lacinemathequedetoulouse.com
ⓔ contact@lacinemathequedetoulouse.com ⓝ Metro: Capitole

### Église Saint Pierre des Cuisines

The crypt under this church is the oldest building in southwest
France. The church above it has been fully restored and is today
a 400-seat auditorium where regular classical concerts are held.
Check with the tourist office or directly at the church for times
and prices of concerts. ⓐ 12 Place Saint Pierre ⓣ (05) 61 22 31 44
ⓔ martine.lacanal@mairie-toulouse.fr ⓛ 10.00–12.00,
14.00–19.00 Mon ⓝ Metro: Capitole. Admission charge

### Espace Croix Baragnon

A contemporary cultural centre that is often used for large
festivals in the city, such as Rio Loco (see page 12). Photography
exhibitions are also regularly staged. ⓐ 24 rue Croix Baragnon
ⓣ (05) 62 27 60 60 ⓔ espace.croix-baragnon@mairie-toulouse.fr
ⓛ 12.00–19.00 Tues–Sat ⓝ Metro: Esquirol

### Galerie de la Halle aux Poissons

Tucked away down a side street next to the Garonne river and
the Pont Neuf bridge, this is a funky young gallery dedicated
mainly to street art and graffiti. ⓐ 11 descente de la Halle
aux Poissons ⓣ (05) 61 52 67 08 ⓦ www.ghp-galerie.com
ⓔ galerie@ghp-galerie.com ⓛ 10.00–20.00 ⓝ Metro: Capitole,
then 10 min walk

---

◗ *The Hotel d'Assézat, home to the Fondation Bemberg*

## Musée des Augustins

This beautiful space is worth visiting for any number of reasons – not least the exhibitions of Renaissance paintings and artefacts, with sculptures dating back to the Middle Ages. From within the museum, you can also access the Augustins Convent, a 14th century church and cloister. It is a peaceful, beautiful spot that provides a lovely break in a busy day's sightseeing. ⓐ 21 rue de Metz ⓣ (05) 61 22 21 82 ⓦ www.augustins.org ⓛ 10.00–18.00 Thur–Mon, 10.00–21.00 Wed, closed Tues ⓝ Metro: Esquirol. Admission charge

## Musée Paul Dupuy

Museum of decorative and graphic arts. The selection is eclectic and goes right up to the present day. ⓐ 13 rue de la Pleau ⓣ (05) 61 14 65 50 ⓔ musee.paul.dupuy@mairie-toulouse.fr ⓛ 10.00–18.00 June–Sept; 10.00–17.00 Wed–Mon, Sept–June ⓝ Metro: Esquirol. Admission charge, students free

## Musée Saint Raymond

Well located by the basilica, this houses archaeology and art from the Middle Ages. ⓐ Place Saint Sernin ⓣ (05) 61 22 31 44 ⓔ saint-raymond@mairie-toulouse.fr ⓛ 10.00–18.00, Sept–June, 10.00–19.00 July–Aug ⓝ Metro: Capitole, then 10 min walk. Admission charge

## Musée du Vieux Toulouse

Housed in a 16th century *hôtel particulier*, this concentrates on everyday objects that formed part of the history of a city as it developed, including old writing implements, stamps, ceramics, drinking vessels and the like. It is due to reopen in May 2008 after refurbishment. ⓐ 7 rue du May ⓣ (05) 62 27 11 50

● *Enjoy art and archaeology at the Musée Saint Raymond*

ⓦ www.toulouse-tourisme.com ⓛ 09.00–12.00, 14.00–18.00
Tues–Sat, closed Sun & Mon ⓝ Metro: Capitole. Admission charge

## RETAIL THERAPY

The Old Town in Toulouse really is a shopper's paradise. You'll
stumble across countless interesting places, from quirky vintage
clothes stores to the latest chic styles from local designers on
their way up to Paris couture.

**Antoine et Lili** Eastern-influenced clothes, and a great place
to pick up beautifully packaged candles, shoes, jewellery and
notebooks, all in luscious pinks, blues and yellows. ⓐ 33 rue Croix
Baragnon ⓣ (05) 62 17 23 14 ⓦ www.altribu.com ⓛ 10.00–19.00
Mon–Sat ⓝ Metro: Esquirol

**Diesel** A large branch of this popular international boutique, and a good place to head to for stylish jeans, and unusual jackets and tops. **ⓐ** 4 rue Saint Antoine **ⓣ** (05) 61 22 82 30 **ⓦ** www.diesel.com **ⓛ** 10.00–19.30 Mon–Sat **ⓝ** Metro: Capitole

**FNAC** The best place to buy CDs, DVDs, cameras and telephones. Also has an internet café and regular photography exhibitions. **ⓐ** 1 Place Capitole **ⓣ** (08) 92 35 06 66 **ⓦ** www.fnac.com **ⓛ** 10.00–19.30 Mon–Sat **ⓝ** Metro: Capitole

## MARKETS

Besides the excellent covered markets of Victor Hugo and Place des Carmes, open every day except Monday, there are plenty of smaller ones happening through the week. On Tuesday and Saturday mornings, there's an organic food market in Place du Capitole. If you're looking for antiques and one-off furniture pieces, there are good markets held around the St Sernin basilica on Saturday and Sunday mornings, while antique book lovers should head to St Aubin on Sunday mornings. For original presents from young artists, try Place Dupuy on the first and third Friday and Saturday of every month, except August. In winter, making the most of local southwestern duck products, Place du Parlement has a *foie gras market* on Wednesday and Friday mornings. If you're after a good selection of local wines and knowledgeable advice, visit the wine merchant at the far end of the Marché Victor Hugo.

**Hall 2** A trendy clothes shop, with a mix of international and one-off local designers. Young friendly staff. Can be expensive, but you'll walk out with something no-one else will be wearing. ⓐ 32 rue des Marchands ⓣ (05) 61 52 92 04 ⓛ 10.00–19.00 Mon–Sat ⓝ Metro: Esquirol

**Imaginarium** Imaginative children's toys at this store – modern and educational, well made and with fun touches like different sized doors for children and adult shoppers. ⓐ 40 rue de Metz ⓣ (05) 61 52 50 23 ⓦ www.imaginarium.fr ⓛ 10.00–19.00 Mon–Sat ⓝ Metro: Capitole

**Nicolas** The wine shop that is now spreading over much of England started out in France, and this is a particularly well stocked store. ⓐ 6 Place Victor Hugo ⓣ (05) 61 22 18 96 ⓦ www.nicolas.com ⓛ 09.00–19.30 Mon–Sat; 10.00–13.00 Sun ⓝ Metro: Jean-Jaurès; Bus: 42

**Ombres Blanches** Complete heaven for book lovers. Great selection of titles, many in English, on everything from arts and poetry to travel. Wide range of contemporary and classic authors. Regular author readings. ⓐ 50 rue Gambetta ⓣ (05) 34 45 53 33 ⓦ www.ombres-blanches.fr ⓛ 10.00–19.00 Mon–Sat ⓝ Metro: Capitole

**Violettes & Pastels** Pick up some violet soaps and fragrances from this smart shop. Good for presents. ⓐ 10 rue St-Pantaléon ⓣ (05) 61 22 14 22 ⓦ www.violettesetpastels.com ⓛ 10.00–19.00 Mon–Sat ⓝ Metro: Capitole

## TAKING A BREAK

Toulouse is a foodie city par excellence. Coffee shops and salons de thé (tea shops) can be found on practically every corner, and there are an increasing number of sushi bars, tapas bars and other exotic types of cuisine.

**L'Autre Salon de Thé £** ❶ Discreet café restaurant that has some of the best cakes you'll find in the city. ⓐ 45 rue des Tourneurs ❶ (05) 61 22 11 63 🕒 11.00–19.00 Ⓝ Metro: Esquirol

**Bapz £** ❷ Cheerful and popular tea house with the full range of English scones and cakes. ⓐ 13 rue de la Bourse ❶ (05) 61 23 06 63 🕒 12.00–19.00 Ⓝ Metro: Esquirol

## AFTER DARK

### RESTAURANTS

Hot spots are centred around Place Saint Georges, Place President Wilson and Place du Capitole, but the countless small streets in between all hold their own treasures.

**Au Père Louis £–££** ❸ A local institution that has been serving up food and drink for nearly a century. ⓐ 45 rue des Tourneurs ❶ (05) 61 21 33 45 🕒 12.00–14.00, 19.00–22.30 Ⓝ Metro: Esquirol

**Mas Y Mas £–££** ❹ Tapas and Basque cider unite with latino music to make this casual bar and restaurant supremely welcoming. Just by Place des Carmes. ⓐ 10 rue des Filatiers

🔺 *Terrasse Daurade in the historic old town*

**☎** (05) 61 25 97 97 **🕐** 12.00–14.30, 19.30–late, closed Sun lunchtime
**Ⓝ** Bus: 38, 54; Metro: Esquirol, then 5 min walk

**La Réserve £–££ ❺** Large windows create an airy, welcoming
and modern space. Good range of pizzas and pastas. **ⓐ** 8 rue
Jean Suau **☎** (05) 61 21 84 00 **🕐** 12.00–14.30, 19.00–22.30
**Ⓝ** Bus: 54, 56; Metro: Esquirol, then 10 min walk

**La Braisière ££ ❻** Right next to Place des Carmes, this lovely
brasserie has red brick walls and wood beams, and cooks
meat over an open fire. Terrace in summer. **ⓐ** 42 rue Pharaon
**☎** (05) 61 52 37 13 **Ⓦ** www.labraisiere.fr **Ⓝ** Bus: 38, 54;
Metro: Esquirol, then 5 min walk

**La Cave au Cassoulet ££ ❼** Traditional, welcoming restaurant that claims to make the city's most authentic version of this famous local dish. ⓐ 54 rue Peyrolières ⓣ (05) 56 13 60 30 ⓛ 12.00–14.00, 19.00–22.00; closed Tues all day plus Wed & Thurs lunchtime Ⓝ Bus: 54, 56; Metro: Esquirol, then 10 min walk

**Brasserie des Beaux-Arts ££–£££ ❽** Next to the Pont Neuf bridge, this is the place to come for seafood platters and to watch locals enjoy their evening aperitif. ⓐ 1 Quai de la Daurade ⓣ (05) 61 21 12 12 ⓛ 12.00–14.00, 19.00–23.00 Ⓝ Bus: 54, 56; Metro: Esquirol, then 10 min walk

**Jardins de l'Opéra £££ ❾** Chef Dominique Toulousy has made this restaurant one of the most sought after (and expensive) in the city. ⓐ 1 Place du Capitole ⓣ (05) 61 23 07 76 ⓦ www.lesjardinsdelopera.com ⓛ 12.00–14.00, 20.00–22.00, closed Sun & Mon Ⓝ Metro: Capitole

## BARS & CLUBS

If you're up for a good time, Toulouse can provide it. This is just a small selection of the many bars, clubs and cafés that go on long into the night. Most don't even start filling up until 23.00, so don't set your alarm clock too early.

**La Cale Sèche** Crowded, smoky, fun bar just off Place du Capitole, specialising in all types of lethal rums. Inside it is dark and dingy, with lots of exposed wood beams and a long wooden bar. ⓐ 41 rue Gambetta ⓛ 19.30–01.30 Mon & Tues, 13.00–01.30 Wed–Sat Ⓝ Metro: Capitole

**The Cockpit** Toulouse's hippest dance spot attracts a mixed crowd. Dance here until the very early hours. 🅰 1 rue du Puits-Vert 🆃 (05) 61 21 87 53 🕒 21.00–04.00 Ⓝ Metro: Capitole

**Le Mandala** Jazz club with weekly live music shows. In summer, there's a terrace here that is perfect for chilling out with a long cold drink. 🅰 23 rue des Amidonniers. 🆃 (05) 6121 10 05 Ⓦ www.lemandala.com 🕒 19.30–late, depending on programme Ⓝ Bus: 1 to Avenue Paul Sejourner

**Senso** Popular with the thirty-something crowd, this sleek bar not far from Place President Wilson is open until dawn. 🅰 6 rue Bayard 🕒 20.00–late Ⓝ Metro: Jean-Jaurès

**La Strada** One of Toulouse's biggest, liveliest night clubs. 🅰 2–4 rue Gabrielle-Péri 🆃 (05) 62 73 11 59 🕒 22.00–dawn Ⓝ Metro: Jean-Jaurès

**Ubu Club** Late night club with a grown-up clientele, enjoying the red velvet seating and happy house music. 🅰 16 rue St Rome 🆃 (05) 61 23 26 75 Ⓦ www.ubu-club.com 🕒 21.00–02.00 Ⓝ Metro: Capitole

**Le Velane** Baroque-style bar with lively jazz music most weekends. 🅰 3 Place Montoulieu, Grand Rond 🆃 (05) 61 53 60 56 Ⓦ www.levelane.com 🕒 Opening times vary. Adjoining bar Caffé Velane closes 02.00 Mon–Fri and 04.00 Sat Ⓝ Metro: St-Cyprien-République

# Île Ramier & the Left Bank

The Garonne divides near Saint-Michel bridge, creating the two branches that embrace Ramier Island. In the middle are three huge complexes: the Parc des Expositions, the Stadium and Ramier Park. The two branches of the river come together again near Empalot, close to the Science Faculties and Pech-David hill. On the far side stretches the Left Bank, with its rising property values and increasingly chic *quartiers* (districts). The Left Bank is the bohemian artists' corner, centred around a fantastic museum of modern art, and with a number of other interesting bars and galleries. Saint Cyprien is a particularly lively, up-and-coming area.

◉ *View of the Dome de l'Hopital de la Grave throught the Pont des Catalan*

## SIGHTS & ATTRACTIONS

### Dôme de la Grave

Part of another working hospital complex, the striking feature for visitors here is a large copper dome that contains a circular chapel. Dating from the 18th century, you can visit the interior, with its ceiling stretching 50 metres above your head. To get to it, you walk through four attractive inner courtyards. ⓐ Place Lange ⓣ (05) 61 77 78 33 ⓝ Metro: St-Cyprien-République

### Hippodrome de la Cepière

Horse racing and casino. The course and surrounding greenery cover 34 hectares and there are 53 race meetings per year. ⓐ 1 chemin des Courses ⓣ (05) 61 49 27 24 ⓦ www.hippodrome-toulouse.com ⓔ contact@hippodrome-toulouse.com ⓝ Metro: Patte-d'Oie

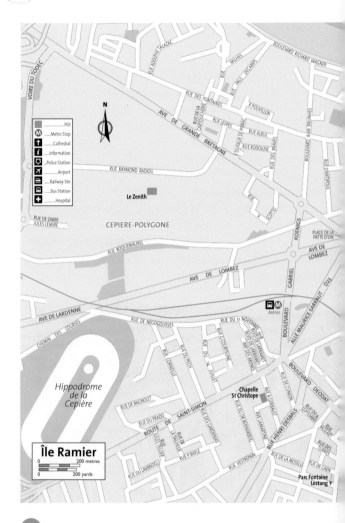

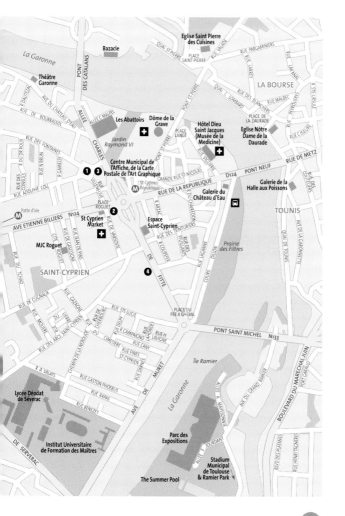

### Hôtel Dieu Saint Jacques

Built in the 12th century, this was originally a stop for pilgrims along the Route de Saint Jacques de Compostelle before becoming Toulouse's first large hospital. Today, some of it is still an active hospital, while other parts are open for exploring, including the lovely gardens, and a first floor balcony with views of the river. ⓐ 2 rue Biguerie ⓣ (05) 61 77 82 33 Ⓝ Metro: St-Cyprien-République

### Jardin Raymond VI

Right on the banks of the Garonne, behind Les Abattoirs modern art museum (see below), this is one of the liveliest city parks. Every weekend it is full of families enjoying the large children's play area, and spilling out from the gallery to enjoy the view of the river as water cascades over the weir. Good jogging and cycling paths along the river at this point also. ⓐ 76 allée Charles de Fitte Ⓝ Bus: 1; Metro: St-Cyprien-République, then 10 min walk

### Parc des Expositions (Exhibition Centre)

Regular events from antiques fairs to sports meetings are held at this large exhibition centre on the Île Ramier. ⓐ Rond Point Michel Benech ⓣ (05) 62 25 45 45 ⓦ www.toulouseexpo.com ⓔ info@toulouseexpo.com Ⓝ Bus: 12, 52 (Left Bank); Metro: Les Arènes then Bus: 31

### Parc Fontaine Lestang

Small but well maintained park in an increasingly chic neighbourhood. ⓐ Rue Fieux ⓛ 07.45–dusk Ⓝ Metro: Mermoz

## Prairie des Filtres

Large green park along the banks of the Garonne. It gets busy at lunchtime with picnicking locals. Sporting events, festivals, concerts and firework displays are often held here. ⓐ Cours Dillon ⓝ Metro: St-Cyprien-République

## Ramier Park

This recreation ground is part of the exhibition centre and stadium complex, and is often full of city sports team and amateur rugby players practising on weekend mornings. It stretches along the length of the island. ⓐ Ramier Island ⓛ 07.00–dusk ⓝ Bus: 12, 52 (Left Bank)

## CULTURE

## Les Abattoirs

Since its opening in 2000, this has become one of France's most exciting contemporary art museums. Housed in a disused 19th century abattoir, its cavernous rooms contain a mass of sculptures, installations and works of art. The collection comprises over 2000 works, including painting, sculpture, mixed media and multimedia by artists from 44 countries. ⓐ 76 allées Charles-de-Fitte ⓣ (05) 62 48 58 00 ⓦ www.lesabattoirs.org ⓔ info@lesabattoirs.org ⓛ 12.00–20.00 Tues–Sun (summer); 11.00–19.00 Tues–Sun (winter) ⓝ Metro: St-Cyprien-République; Bus: 1. Admission charge

🔺 *The striking Musee des Abbattoirs, museum of modern art*

### Centre Municipal de l'Affiche, de la Carte Postale et de l'Art Graphique

An art centre for posters, postcards and graphic arts that not only sells a number of excellent cards but also has a large collection of illustrations from comic books and more traditional artistic outlets. The building also contains a library, video library and workshops. ⓐ 58 allées Charles-de-Fitte ⓣ (05) 61 59 24 64 ⓔ centre.affiche@mairie-toulouse.fr ⓛ 09.00–12.00, 14.00–18.00 Mon–Fri Ⓜ Metro: St-Cyprien-République; Bus: 1

### Chapelle St Christophe

Small Catholic chapel with some intricate carvings on its interior and exterior walls. ⓐ Ave Lamartine Ⓜ Metro: Fontaine-Lestang

### Espace Saint-Cyprien

Large contemporary arts space with music, theatre, the Chapeau Rouge bar and an art gallery of photography and sculpture.  56 allées Charles-de-Fitte  (05) 61 22 27 77  Metro: Saint-Cyprien-République; Bus: 1, 3, 14

### Galerie du Château d'Eau

One of Toulouse's most unusual and rewarding galleries, this contemporary photographer's gallery is housed in a water tower. The exhibitions change frequently, and often deal with a specific theme such as alienation or global warming, with numerous different photographers giving their take on a single issue.  1 place Laganne  (05) 61 77 09 40  www.galeriechateaudeau.org  chateaudeau@galeriechateaudeau.org  13.00–19.00 Tues–Sun  Metro: St-Cyprien-République. Admission charge, under 18s free

### M J C Roguet

Exhibition space with ever-evolving range of contemporary artists, mainly sculpture and projected imagery.  9 rue de Gascogne  (05) 61 77 26 00  11.00–18.00 Tues–Sat  Metro: Patte-d'Oie  www.mjcroguet.com  mjc.roguet@wanadoo.fr

### Musée de la Medicine

Interesting and unusual museum looking specifically at medical development in Toulouse. You'll find a collection of gruesome medical instruments as well as sculptures and paintings.  Hôtel Dieu Saint Jacques, 2 Rue Viguerie, Pont Neuf  (05) 61 77 84 25  http://museemedecine.free.fr  arielle.auvergnat@neuf.fr  12.00–18.00 Wed–Sun  Metro: St-Cyprien-République

### Théâtre Garonne

This 250-seat theatre provides a stage for many visiting theatre groups and contemporary productions. ⓐ 1 ave du Château d'Eau ⓣ (05) 62 48 54 77 ⓦ www.theatregaronne.com ⓔ info@theatregaronne.com ⓝ Metro: St-Cyprien-République

## RETAIL THERAPY

It can take some digging around to find the best shops over on this side of the river, but it is fantastic for bargains, more unusual food stuffs and creations by young artists and designers. There is a collection of interesting regional and exotic food shops, and new boutiques are springing up all the time – a clear sign of how dynamic this area has become. The best market is held in Saint Cyprien, but you'll often find the smaller squares attract a smattering of local stalls selling photographs, organic produce or music.

### Saint Cyprien and Patte-d'Oie

Bustling local neighbourhood with everything from pet stores to delicatessens to small clothing boutiques. A great place for finding exotic ingredients for Thai or Indian curries. Historically, this area was subject to frequent flooding, and as such attracted the poor, sick or immigrant communities that the more affluent parts of town rejected. All that has changed, and with the arrival of the metro house prices have been rocketing and the excellent shops have been moving in. The mains shops are centred around Rue de la République and Place de la Patte d'Oie. ⓝ Metro: Patte-d'Oie

**Place de la Patte d'Oie** This area was originally called Reine Pédauque, after a Roman aqueduct that used to exist here. In the Occitan language, *pédauque* became *patte d'oie*. Today it is a bustling intersection of three major roads, and the site of some good cafés. Ⓝ Metro: Patte-d'Oie

**St Cyprien Market** A picturesque and popular market, held every morning except Mondays. A wide range of local food producers set up their stalls within the original *halle* (market hall). ⓐ Place Roguet Ⓛ 07.00–13.00 Ⓝ Metro: St-Cyprien-République

Ⓞ *Deliciously nutty nougat from Toulouse*

## TAKING A BREAK

Increasingly trendy bars and restaurants are centred
around Place St Cyprien, Place de la Patte d'Oie and
Rue de la République.

**Bar le Ravelin £ ❶** Open from very early until very late, making
this bustling, friendly and a great meeting place. Piano music
some evenings. **ⓐ** 6 place du Ravelin **ⓣ** (05) 61 42 93 32
**ⓛ** 07.00–02.00 **Ⓝ** Metro: St-Cyprien-République

**Le Bistrot des Halles Saint Cyprien £–££ ❷** Friendly and
popular café bar and bistro with good food at excellent
prices. **ⓐ** 17 Place Roguet, Saint Cyprien **ⓣ** (05) 62 48 93 86
**ⓛ** 07.00–22.30 **Ⓝ** Metro: Patte-d'Oie

## AFTER DARK

### RESTAURANTS
**Ecuries d'Athena ££ ❸** Local specialities including a very good
cassoulet. Some vegetarian options also. Small terrace garden
at the back. Good wine list of over 400 bottles, and you can
go into the cellar and pick your own bottle. **ⓐ** 65 allées
Charles-de-Fitte **ⓣ** (05) 61 59 77 11 **ⓦ** www.ecuriesathena.com
**ⓛ** 12.00–14.00, 19.30–22.00 Mon–Fri, 19.30–22.00 Sat, closed Sun
**Ⓝ** Metro: St-Cyprien-République

**Le Petit Diable Brasserie ££** ❹ A place for meat lovers. Chargrilled steaks that are practically alive on the plate. ⓐ 99 allées Charles-de-Fitte ❶ (05) 61 42 86 95 ⓛ 12.00–14.00, 19.00–22.30 Ⓜ Metro: St-Cyprien-République

## BARS & CLUBS

**Le Chapeau Rouge** Concerts and DJ nights are held most weeks at this hip venue. ⓐ 56 allées Charles-de-Fitte ❶ (05) 61 22 27 77 ⓔ lechapeaurouge@mairie-toulouse.fr ❶ Enquire for concert dates Ⓜ Metro: St-Cyprien-République

**Hall 7, Parc Expo** International DJs regularly play in this cavernous space, perfect for massive club nights. ⓐ Île du Ramier ❶ 08 92 68 36 22 / 08 92 39 01 00 ⓛ 22.00 til late, on club nights (always check ahead) Ⓜ Bus: 12, 52 (Left Bank)

**Le Kléo/Le Ramier** Club nights with experimental DJs, from punk and disco to house. ⓐ 1 ave du Grand Ramier, Île du Ramier ❶ (05) 61 52 86 63 ❶ 22.00–late on club nights (always check ahead) Ⓜ Bus: 12, 52 (Left Bank)

**Le Zénith** The biggest stadium in France, with seating for 9,000 people. Its size and glamorous architecture means it has no problem attracting big international names. Club nights are also held here regularly. ⓐ 11 ave Raymond Badiou ❶ (05) 62 74 49 49 ❶ Times vary, always check ahead Ⓜ Metro: Patte-d'Oie or Arénes

# The Boulevards & further afield

Outside of the Old City, there is still plenty to see. The Boulevards that ring Toulouse follow the course of the canal, and have various access points on to the tow path. And as you get further out from downtown you'll experience the change from traditional to high tech Toulouse, as the aeronautical and space industries are based out here.

## SIGHTS & ATTRACTIONS

### Aerothèque

A comprehensive exhibition of the history of aeronautics in Toulouse. ⓐ 18 Rue Montmorency ⓣ (05) 61 93 93 57 ⓦ www.aerotheque.fr ⓔ aerotheque@wanadoo.fr ⓛ 14.00–17.00 Wed; closed Aug ⓝ Bus: 15 to Compans Caffarelli gardens. Admission charge

### Les Ailes Anciennes

This is where old airplanes go to die, or rather to be gazed at by enthusiastic plane spotters. Booking is compulsory. ⓐ Poste de Garde Louis Bréguet, Colomiers ⓣ (05) 61 21 70 01 ⓦ www.aatlse.org ⓔ contact@aatlse.org ⓛ Guided tours 09.30 and 10.30 Sat ⓝ Train: Colomiers Gare. Admission charge

### Arnaud-Bernard

Pretty part of town near Jardin Compans Caffarelli, with some interesting shops to explore. To the west, wander into Saint Pierre and Amidonniers, and down to the Garonne river.

● *Aeronautical and high-tech Toulouse*

### Amphithéâtre Romain de Purpan

Built around the 1st century, one of the best ways to explore this well preserved amphitheatre is by guided tour on a Sunday. Booking is required. Gladiator conquests were held here until the end of the 4th century and the tour gives you plenty of gruesome stories. ⓐ Ave des Arènes Romaines ⓣ (05) 61 22 31 44 ⓦ www.arena-stadium.eu.org ⓛ 14.00–18.00 Sun, June & Sept; 14.00–19.00 Sun; July–Aug ⓝ Bus: 66 to Cauterets, 70 to rue de Purpan. Admission charge

### Canal du Midi

See feature on page 18.

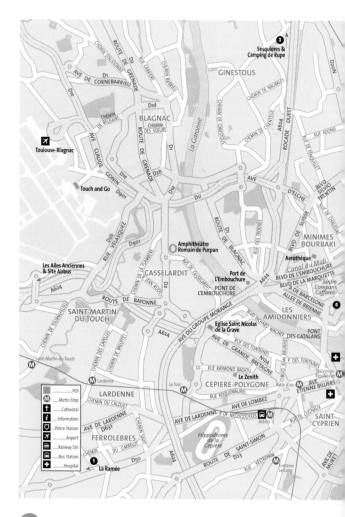

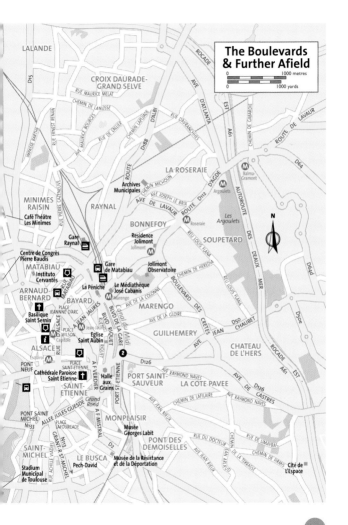

## The Boulevards & Further Afield

| 0 | | 1000 metres |
| 0 | | 1000 yards |

### Centre de Congrès Pierre Baudis

Beautiful glass and stainless steel building, an interesting
stop on a walking tour of the city. 11 espl Compans Caffarelli
(05) 62 30 40 40 www.centre-congres-toulouse.fr
Bus: 15, 70, 71

### Cité de L'Espace

Toulouse's space park, where you look round a replica of the MIR
space station, watch movies at the IMAX theatre, play games and
visit a more serious exhibition showcasing how satellite phones
work. See what is just around the corner for the communication
industry. For younger children, there's an excellent Young
Astronauts play area, where the slide comes out of a huge play
rocket. Parc de la Plaine, ave Jean Gonord (05) 62 71 48 71
www.cite-espace.com contact@cite-espace.com
09.00–18.00 Mon–Fri, 09.00–19.00 Sat & Sun Bus: 19, 35;
Metro: Marengo then Bus: 31. Admission charge

### Église Saint Aubin

A handsome catholic church dating from the 13th century,
standing in the middle of a very pleasant large square.
Every Sunday there's a good market in this increasingly
sought-after neighbourhood. Place St Aubin (05) 61 63 77 31
http://catholique-toulouse.cef.fr Metro: Jean-Jaurès, then
walk along rue de la Comobette towards Boulevard Riquet

### Église Saint Nicolas de la Grave

Large orthodox church with an attractive façade and
lovely stained glass inside. 302 ave de Grande-Bretagne

📞 (05) 61 31 92 25  ✉ serge.pescay@free.fr  🕐 Service at 17.30 Sat
Ⓜ Metro: Patte d'Oie plus a 10 min walk

## Jardin Compans Caffarelli

Ten hectares of park, with a Japanese garden that gives access
to the Canal du Midi. The artificial hills, raked gravel geometric
designs, wooden bridge and teahouse all create a magical
atmosphere. At the far end of the park there's a large lake,
which has a children's playground and a refreshments kiosk.
🅰 Blvd Lascrosses  🕐 07.45–18.00  Ⓜ Bus: 15, 70, 71

## Jolimont Observatoire

The observatory was built in 1846 and today, although no
longer used, is open to visitors and school groups. It has lovely,

---

### THE 'GREEN LUNGS' OF TOULOUSE

Bookmarking the city to the north, south, east and west
are four large green spaces, collectively known as the
city's *zones vertes* (green spaces). They make relaxing days
or afternoons out, and are good for dog walking, picnics
or jogging. Les Argoulets, to the east, has 45 hectares of
rugby and baseball pitches with judo space and an ice rink.
Pech-David, to the south, is a 270 hectare park overlooking
the Garonne river. La Ramée, to the west, is 280 hectares
and has a large fishing lake, sailing lake and archery range.
Sesquieres, to the north, is a 117 hectare park with water
skiing on the lake in summer time.

tumbledown gardens all around, and is rather ramshackle, but it is great fun for children. The view from the dome on Friday nights can be breathtaking. ⓐ 1 ave Camille Flammarion ⓣ (05) 61 58 42 01 ⓦ www.imcce.fr ⓔ sap@easynet.fr ⓛ Gardens: 07.45–18.00; Observatory Dome: 21.00 Fri for a free tour ⓝ Metro: Jolimont

### La Péniche Maison de la Violette (Violet House Barge)

An unusual experience can be had on board the Violet House barge. Violets, in flower from November to March, have been grown in Toulouse for 150 years. This permanently moored barge is part museum, part shop devoted entirely to the flowers. It sells a range of all things violet – from honey to marmalade, tea, perfumes and shower gels. ⓐ Blvd de Bonrepos ⓣ (05) 61 99 01 30 ⓦ www.lamaisondelaviolette.fr ⓛ 14.00–19.00 Mon, 10.00–12.30, 14.00–19.00 Tues–Sat, closed second week of January ⓝ Metro: Marengo; Bus: 15, 16, 22, 21, 41

### Site Airbus & Clement Adler

The largest aeronautical site in Europe is open to visitors for guided tours by prior appointment only. You can tour both the double decker Airbus and a model of the original Concorde. Booking is compulsory. ⓐ 10 ave Guynemer, Colomiers ⓣ (05) 61 18 06 01 ⓦ www.taxiway.fr ⓔ reservation@taxiway.fr ⓛ Mon–Sat ⓝ Train to Colomiers Gare. Admission charge

▶ *Airbus has brought much employment to the city*

### Touch and Go

Find out what goes on behind the scenes of an airport, from checking in bags to retrieving lost luggage. Guided tours for groups only. Booking is compulsory. Aérogare Aviation d'Affaires, Blagnac (05) 61 71 62 11 http://touchandgo.free.fr jeanluc@touchandgo.free.fr Mon–Sat Bus: Navette Aéroport, 17, 66. Admission charge

## CULTURE

### Archives Municipales

Documentation centre that contains some interesting old photos of the city. There are also good historical picture books for sale in the shop. 2 rue des Archives (05) 61 61 63 33 www.archives.mairie-toulouse.fr archives@mairie-toulouse.fr. 09.00–17.00 Mon–Fri Metro: Roseraie

### Café Théâtre Les Minimes

Theatre and bar with a range of excellent smaller productions. Well worth the trip out to the far side of the Boulevards, north of the centre. 6 rue Gélibert (05) 62 72 06 36 www.lesminimes.com contact@lesminimes.com Shows: 21.00 Mon–Fri, 20.00 & 22.00 Sat Bus: 10. Admission charge for shows

### Halle aux Grains

Hexagonal concert hall and exhibition space that sees a lively contemporary arts programme throughout the year, from visiting pianists to operas. The Orchestre du Capitole has its base here.

The building itself was a covered market used for trading cereals from 1864 until 1952, when it became a sports centre. It was finally converted into a concert hall in 1974. Place Dupuy (05) 61 63 13 13 www.onct.mairie-toulouse.fr Opening hours vary, depending on programme. Call ahead for details. Bus: 16; Metro: Jean-Jaurès, then 10 min walk

### Instituto Cervantès

A cultural space dedicated to Spanish and Basque culture. Almost all exhibitions are presented in both Spanish and French. 31 rue des Chalets (05) 61 62 48 64 http://toulouse.cervantes.es difusion@cervantes.es 10.00–15.00 Mon–Fri; closed Aug Bus: 61, 42

### Le Médiathèque José Cabanis

A strikingly modern building, and a welcome piece of architecture amid the sprawl of Toulouse's outer boulevards. It contains an arts centre, a media library named after José Cabanis (a writer from Toulouse who died in 2000), and hosts a wide range of cultural and leisure activities for adults and teenagers. There are some early learning activities for children. You will also find a fantastic documentary collection in every possible format, from books to CDs, videos, DVDs and online. 1 allée Jacques Chaban-Delmas (05) 62 27 40 00 10.00–19.00 Tues, Wed, Fri & Sat; 14.00–19.00 Thurs; 14.00–18.00 Sun www.bibliothequedetoulouse.fr contact@bibliothequedetoulouse.fr Metro: Marengo. Admission charge, under 18s free

🔺 *Japanese art at Musée Georges Labit*

### Musée Georges Labit

Unusual works of art at this intimate museum, concentrating almost entirely on Asia and Ancient Egypt. 🅰 17 rue du Japon 🕿 (05) 61 14 65 50 🅔 musee.georges.labit@mairie-toulouse.fr 🕙 10.00–17.00 Wed–Mon 🇳 Bus: 78, 79, 80. Admission charge

### Musée de la Résistance et de la Déportation

Part museum, part memorial, part research centre, this collection is centred around Toulouse and southwest France during World War II. Expect plenty of honest exhibits about collaboration as well as the resistance movement. 🅰 52 allée des Demoiselles 🕿 (05) 61 14 80 40 🅔 gagullo@yahoo.fr 🕙 09.30–12.00, 14.00–18.00 Mon–Fri, 14.00–17.00 Sat 🇳 Bus: 10, 78, 79, 80

## RETAIL THERAPY

Once you get out to the Boulevards and beyond, a lot of the best shopping is centred around the commercial centres. Although less romantic than downtown, parking is easy and many of the best shops are located in one space.

**La Cave Spirituelle** Wine shop with wide choice of regional bottles and exceptionally helpful staff. Delivery available also – free locally for orders above 75 euros. 🄰 21 place Arnaud Bernard ☎ (05) 61 22 64 55 🌐 www.wines-and-spirits.com 🕙 10.00–12.30, 15.00–19.30 Mon–Sat 🅜 Metro: Jeanne d'Arc or Compans Caffarelli

**Centre Commercial Compans** Large centre with a variety of clothes and interior shops, plus a FNAC for concert tickets. 🄰 3 Espl Compans Caffarelli 🅜 Bus: 60, 61, 69; Metro: Compans Caffarelli

**Centre Commercial, Portet-sur-Garonne** The largest in Toulouse, with a wide variety of international and local shops. 🄰 Carrefour, blvd de l'Europe, 31120 Portet-sur-Garonne ☎ (05) 61 72 10 51

**Cultura** Music, books and technology at this well stocked store. 🄰 12 Boulevard de l'Europe (opposite Carrefour), Portet sur Garonne ☎ (05) 61 72 39 48 🌐 www.cultura.com 🅜 Bus: 47, 49 to Portet Gare

**Imaginarium** A large branch of this fantastic children's store, with modern educational games and toys. 🄰 Centre Commercial Carrefour, Portet sur Garonne ☎ (05) 62 20 25 84 🌐 www.imaginarium.fr 🕙 10.00–19.00 Mon–Sat 🅜 Bus: 47, 49 to Portet Gare

**Marché du Boulevard de Strasbourg** Lively market selling fruit, vegetables and a wide variety of foodstuffs. blvd de Strasbourg 07.00–11.00 Metro: Jean-Jaurès

## TAKING A BREAK

**L'Art de Vivre £** ❶ Five minutes from the airport at Blagnac, this is a sophisticated, welcoming restaurant with an attractive leafy terrace. 279 chem Ramelet Moundi, Tournefeuille (05) 61 07 52 52 www.lartdevivre.fr 12.00–14.00, 19.30–22.00 Thur–Sat, 12.00–14.00 Sun–Tues, closed Wed Bus: 63, 21 to Tournefeuille

**Les Copains d'Abord £–££** ❷ Friendly restaurant with an interesting, eclectic menu and choice of Latin American food or classic French bistro style. 38 rue du Pont Guilheméry (05) 62 47 29 99 www.les-copainsdabord.fr les.copains@wanadoo.fr 12.00–14.00, 19.00–22.30 Mon–Fri, 19.00–22.30 Sat; closed Sun, July–Aug Bus: 16

## AFTER DARK

### RESTAURANTS
**Village Gaulois ££** ❸ Family-friendly Asterix-themed restaurant with 2,000 sq m of terrace for sunny days, and rather overpriced food. DJs from 23.00 at weekends. Lac de Sesquières, Allée des Foulques (05) 61 70 37 70 www.levillagegaulois.fr 12.00–14.30, 18.30–22.30 Tues–Sun, open late Fri and Sat

⬢ Narrow streets mean some creative parking in the old town

**Michel Sarran ££ £££** ❹ Good value for a gastronomic, Michelin-starred restaurant. Book ahead, particularly at lunchtime when the whole of the city is trying for their prix fixe menu. ⓐ 21 boulevard Armand Duportal ⓣ (05) 61 12 32 32 ⓦ www.michel-sarran.com ⓛ 12.00–13.45, 20.00–21.45 Mon–Fri; closed Aug ⓝ Bus: 25

## BARS & CLUBS

**Havana Café/Ramonville** Indie nights and visiting bands make this a popular student venue. Alongside the concert venue is a dance club. ⓐ 2 ave des Crêtes, St Agne ⓣ (05) 62 88 34 94 ⓦ www.havana-cafe.fr ⓛ Call ahead for concert times ⓝ Metro: St-Agne-SNCF

**Le Purple** Currently one of the coolest night spots in the city. Big name visiting DJs, but very much a home grown sense of abandon. ⓐ 2 rue Castellane ⓣ (05) 62 73 04 67 ⓦ www.le-purple.com ⓛ 22.00–05.00 Tues–Sat ⓝ Metro: Jean-Jaurès

**Rest'ô Jazz** Lively and charming night spot, with live music and well priced, generous food. ⓐ 8 rue Amélie ⓣ (05) 61 57 96 95 ⓦ www.restojazz.com ⓛ 19.00–02.00 Mon–Sat ⓝ Metro: Marengo

**Casino Salies-du-Salat** Large modern casino complex, with restaurants and slot machines. ⓐ Blvd de Casino, Salies du Salat ⓣ (05) 61 97 06 03 ⓦ www.casinocity.com ⓛ 10.00–04.00 Mon–Fri, 10.00–05.00 Sat & Sun ⓝ Bus: free bus from Matabiau. Admission charge

⏵ *The road to Albi in the Pyrénées*

# The Pyrénées

One of the great things about Toulouse is how close it is to the mountains of the Pyrénées. This means walking, mountain biking and canoeing in summer, and skiing in winter. There are also a number of thermal spa resorts, and plenty of local crafts and dishes to enjoy. As you get closer to the Spanish border, both the dialect and the dishes take on a more southern Mediterranean feeling, and the ability to dip in and out of both countries also makes for a fascinating trip.

## GETTING THERE

The Pyrénées is a huge area, covering 430 km from the Mediterranean to the Atlantic and forming a natural barrier between France and Spain. It is roughly split into three sections – the Pyrénées Atlantiques by Biarritz and the Basque country, the Hautes Pyrénées, and the Pyrénées Orientales towards Roussillon and the Côte d'Azur. From Toulouse, the easiest and quickest section to get to is the Hautes Pyrénées. You can be within its foothills in about an hour from Toulouse, although with a few more days, a lot more is possible.

### By rail

There are many trains that go from Toulouse central railway station to the Haute Garonne and Pyrénées. The most interesting is **Le Train Jaune** (the Yellow Train ⓦ www.trainstouristiques-ter.com/train_jaune.htm), which travels through the Tet valley high into the Pyrénées, then descends into Spain and ends up in Barcelona.

🔺 *Foix's castle dominates the surrounding countryside*

Since 2005, the train itself – although still yellow –
has been modernised.
**SNCF timetable and bookings** Ⓦ www.sncf.com

### By road

Heading out of Toulouse by car, take the A66. The N20 road then
leads you through the Haut Garonne to Foix, the best starting
point for the Ariège valley. For Andorra, continue on N20 road
through Tarascon-sur-Ariège and Aix-les-Thermes, then take
the tiny N2 that winds up through increasingly steep scenery.
Alternatively, for the Atlantic side of the mountain range, take
the A64 from Toulouse, which leads over to Bayonne and Lourdes.

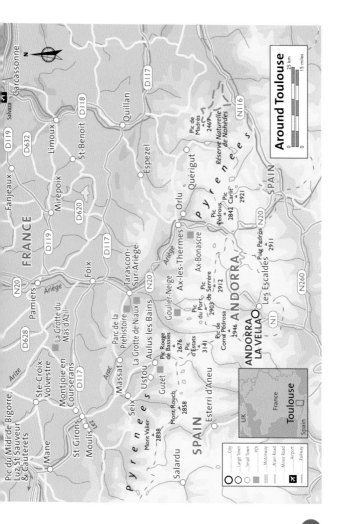

**Around Toulouse**

0 — 25 km
0 — 15 miles

N

FRANCE

Carcassonne
Salvaza
D119
D632
D118
Limoux
D620
St-Benoit
Quillan
D117
Mirepoix
Fanjeaux
D119
D117
Espezel
Pic de Madrès
2469
Réserve Naturelle de Nohèdes
N116
Pamiers
Ariège
Foix
D117
D628
La Grotte du Mas d'Azil
Tarascon-sur-Ariège
N20
Ste-Croix-Volvestre
Arize
Ariège
Orlu
Quérigut
Pic de Madrès
SPAIN
Montjoie en Couserans
Parc de la Préhistoire
Ax-les-Thermes
Pic Pedrous
2842
Pic Carlit
2921
D117
St-Girons
Massat
La Grotte de Niaux
Goulier-Neige
Ax-Bonascre
Pic Pedrous
Mane
Arac
Aulus les Bains
Pic Serrère
2912
ANDORRA
Puig Pedrós
2911
Moulis
Lez
Seix
Pic Rouge de Bassies
2676
Pic du Port
2903
N20
N260
Ustou
Pic d'Estats
3141
Pic de Serrère
2903
Les Escaldès
N1
Pic du Midi de Bigorre, Luz St Sauveur & Cauterets
Pyrénées
Guzet
Mont Rouch
2858
Pic de Coma Pedrosa
2946
ANDORRA LA VELLA
Mont Valier
2838
Esterri d'Aneu
SPAIN
Salardu

Toulouse
UK
France
Spain

City
Large Town
Small Town
POI
Motorway
Main Road
Minor Road
Railway
Airport

Tour buses for travelling from Toulouse throughout the region depart from the Gare Routière (central bus station ⓐ 68 blvd Pierre Sémard ⓣ (05) 61 61 67 67) and from Courriers de la Garonne (ⓐ 133 chemin du Sang de Serp ⓣ (05) 62 72 37 23 ⓔ courriersdelagaronne@connex.net)

## SIGHTS & ATTRACTIONS

### Andorra

The independent principality of Andorra is only 90 minutes from Toulouse and is a duty-free haven, so it makes a good

◓ *Andorra's pistes and ski lift*

day trip to stock up on perfumes and wines or spirits. It is also a base for skiing, with several family-friendly resorts on either side, and there are a number of good restaurants and bars. Since EU borders have become open, border checks by the *douanes volantes* (free-ranging customs officers) have become less frequent. But be aware, as customs officials can stop you for a routine check anywhere they like. Because of the tax-free status of Andorra, checks are regular on the N20 road.

## SKIING

Skiing in the Pyrénées is lower than in the Alps and the slopes are often easier, perfect for beginners and for families. Snowboarding is popular. The first slopes start just over an hour from Toulouse, but the higher you go, the better they are. A few resorts:

**Ax-Bonascre** This is one of the first resorts you come to on the road from Toulouse, and although you cannot rely on the snow at this height, it is popular for its natural hot springs. Take the RN20 road.

**Goulier Neige** One of the higher ski resorts, reaching 1,900 m at its peaks. You'll find a good variety of green, blue and red runs, and there is a (free) snowy playground for children at the foot of the slopes. The resort is 125 km from Toulouse, off the RN20, or 20 km from Tarascon-sur-Ariège railway station.

**Guzet** Right in the middle of the Ariège valley, this is great for families, with a snow park for children. You also get some pretty steep black runs. Take exit 20 from the A64, towards Saint-Girons.

**Cauterets** Well established ski village and popular with young skiers, so the nightlife is more promising here. You approach the slopes by cable car, and there are plenty of non-ski activities, from spas and bowling alleys to ice rinks and late night bars.

### Ariège Valley

Ariège is a picturesque river that flows through the Pyrénées. The main town is Foix, in the foothills, with a large castle that dominates the surrounding scenery.

### Pic du Midi de Bigorre

It is worth the slightly longer drive up into the Vallée des Gaves (Valley of the Mountain Streams) to see one of the Pyrénées' most stirring sights. It is reached by a recently opened cable car, or by the previous option, a four hour hike. ☎ (08) 25 00 28 77 🕐 daily June–Sept; Thur–Mon, Oct–May. Charge for cable car

### Tarascon-sur-Ariège

An attractive town with good restaurants, and the centre for many prehistoric remains in the area. Its Prehistoric Art Park shows how water created the limestone caves that people lived in, how the cave dwellers survived and made tools, and how and why the wall paintings were created. There are good walking tours around the park and children get to try their hand at spear throwing. Booking required. ☎ (05) 61 05 88 37. Admission charge

## CULTURE

### Ariège Aventure

In the middle of the Orlu leisure park, with canoeing, abseiling and tree climbing for children and adults. Six adventure tracks, one canyon. ⓐ Les Forges d'Orlu, Orlu ☎ (05) 61 05 97 33 ⓦ www.ariege-aventure.com ⓔ infos@ariege-aventure.com 🕐 10.00–19.00, July–Sept; 13.00–18.00, Apr–Jun & Oct–Nov;

Feb–Mar on advance booking only (more than 12 people);
closed Dec & Jan. Admission charge

### La Ferme Basque

Unspoilt rural farm with a fantastic view. Try brebis, cheese made
from local ewes' milk. Also serves food, so a good place to stop
for a quick lunch or early evening drink. ⓐ Route du Cambasque,
Cauterets ⓣ (05) 62 92 54 32 ⓦ www.fermebasque.com
ⓔ fermebasque@wanadoo.fr ⓛ Farm: 10.00–19.00, times flexible.
Food served 12.30–14.00, 19.00–20.30, later in July–Aug

### La Grotte du Mas d'Azil

On the banks of the L'Arize river, this huge underground complex
is accessed via a natural tunnel and used to be the sheltering
place of mammoths and rhinoceroses. There's a light and sound
show in the caves, a museum and a 3rd century monolithic chapel.
ⓐ Le Mas d'Azil ⓣ (05) 61 69 97 71 ⓦ www.sesta.fr ⓛ 14.00–18.00
April & May; 10.00–12.00, 14.00–18.00 Jun; 10.00–18.00 July & Aug;
14.00–18.00 Sun only, Sept & Oct; 14.00–18.00 Sun only, March;
closed rest of year. Admission charge

### La Grotte de Niaux

A 12,000 year old cave with detailed pictures of animals that were
hunted, and images of stick people tracking them. Enormously
popular and places are strictly limited, so book this in advance
from the Maison des Midi-Pyrénées office in Toulouse. ⓐ Niaux
ⓣ (05) 61 05 88 37 ⓦ www.niaux.net ⓛ 11 visits per day in July
and August. Two in English: 09.00 and 12.30. Times vary.
Admission charge

## TAKING A BREAK & AFTER DARK

**Bar des Trois Pics £** Specialising in local ingredients, this is a friendly place. Work up an appetite first with the nearby fishing, rock climbing and mountain biking. ⓐ Moulis ⓣ (05) 61 04 85 49 ⓛ 11.00–23.00

**Le Central £** In the pretty village of Seix, this is well located within a short walk of the chateau. There's a lively bar, and a traditional bistro menu. ⓐ Seix ⓣ (05) 61 66 82 02 ⓛ 11.00–22.30

**Le Sacca £** After a hard day's skiing or walking around Cauterets, this is a good place to eat fresh, modern French food. ⓐ Hôtel Astérides Sacca, 11 blvd Latapie-Flurin, Cauterets ⓣ (05) 62 92 50 02 ⓦ www.asterides-sacca.com ⓔ contact@asterides-sacca.com ⓛ 12.00–14.30, 19.00–22.30

**La Grange de l'Agouadis £–££** You might find amateur musicians twanging their guitars here, or gathering round the piano. Even without music, you get to enjoy a varied, relaxed menu from pizzas to salads. ⓐ Martine Papaïx, Aulus les Bains ⓣ (05) 61 96 00 72 ⓦ www.aulus-les-bains.com ⓔ mpapaix@free.fr ⓛ 10.30–24.00

**Le Txoko £–££** In the middle of a lively ski station, this has a restaurant, a pizzeria, a bowling alley and a bar that doubles as a disco during high season. ⓐ 17 ave de Barèges, Esquièze-Sère, Luz St Sauveur ⓣ (05) 62 92 35 57 ⓔ letxoko@aol.com ⓛ 11.00–00.00 year round, later at weekends during ski season

◔ Town houses and the ever-present chateau in Foix

## ACCOMMODATION

### Ariège Valley

**Auberge du Mont Calivert £** Pretty restaurant and hotel in the middle of green countryside. ⓐ Bergerat, Montjoie en Courserans ⓣ (05) 61 96 75 22 ⓔ murielsch@aol.fr ⓛ Food served: 12.00–14.00, 19.00–21.30

**Hôtel Lons ££** Former coaching inn overlooking the river that runs through the centre of Foix. Popular restaurant also. ⓐ 6 pl Georges Dutilh, Foix ⓣ (05) 34 09 28 00 ⓦ www.hotel-lons-foix.com ⓔ hotel-lons-foix@wanadoo.fr ⓛ Food served: 12.00–14.30, 19.00–22.00

### Skiing

**Hôtel le Breilh £** A simple but well equipped 25 bedroom hotel which makes a good base for hiking in the summer and skiing in the winter. ⓐ Place du Breilh, Ax-les-Thermes ⓣ (05) 61 64 24 29 ⓦ www.ariegehotellebreilh.com

**Hôtel les Edelweiss £** Very close to the centre of the town and to the ski lift. ⓐ 7 blvd Latapie Flurin, Cauterets ⓣ (05) 62 92 52 75 ⓦ www.edelweiss-hotel.fr ⓔ reservations@edelweiss-hotel.fr

**Résidence du Haut Couserans ££** Right at the foot at the ski slopes in Guzet, with a friendly restaurant (with all important central fire), good bar, pool and sauna. ⓐ Guzet 1400 ,09140 Ustou ⓣ (05) 34 09 09 09 ⓦ www.sbs-vacances.com ⓔ haut.couserans@wanadoo.fr

# The Vineyards

Toulouse is surrounded by vineyards, and visiting them also makes a good excuse to explore some of the pretty towns and villages in the area. Don't attempt them all at once – rather dip in and out on a few day trips. Take your pick from, amongst others, Gaillac, Fronton, Madiran, Côtes de Saint-Mont, Jurançon, Coteaux du Quercy, Tursan, Côtes du Brulhois, Béarn, Pacherenc du Vic-Bilh, Marcillac, Armagnac, Floc de Gascogne. Not all are covered here – there's just too much to see – so instead we have highlighted a few particularly pretty towns in Tarn that allow easy access to the surrounding vines and other activities. For walking, mountain biking and some lake swimming, the Tarn valley itself is beautiful.

## GETTING THERE

### By rail

Albi is one hour away from Toulouse by train. Trains leave Toulouse central railway station approximately once every hour during the week, and regularly at weekends. The last train from Toulouse to Albi leaves around 22.45. Services are subject to alterations, so always check times beforehand. Ⓦ www.sncf.com

### By road

Albi is around 90 minutes from Toulouse by car, taking the A68 road to the northeast of the city. Gaillac is much closer, just 50 km northeast of Toulouse on the A89 road, taking around 60 minutes by car. Even closer, just a short hop on the A62 towards Bordeaux, is Fronton.

○ *Spectacular Millau Viaduct, the world's tallest vehicular bridge*

There are three buses to and from Toulouse daily, and the journey takes around 90 minutes. See ⓦ www.albibus.com

**Albi central bus station** ❸ Pl Stalingrad, Albi ❶ (05) 63 54 58 61

Tarnbus operates a local bus service around Albi and surrounding areas. ❸ rue Hôtel de Ville, Albi ❶ (05) 63 38 43 43

## SIGHTS & ATTRACTIONS

### Albi

Albi is the capital of the Tarn region, an attractive town with a cathedral, good restaurants and wide streets. The entire place is rich in architectural history, and built in Languedoc-style red

brick, as is Toulouse. Besides its cathedral, Albi is best known as the birth place of the painter Toulouse Lautrec, and you should expect – besides the excellent museum – many of its bars and restaurants to feature frescoes of Moulin Rouge dancers. Many restaurants also offer versions of dishes created by Lautrec, as he was a keen amateur chef.

Information on many of the sights, attractions and events listed here is given by the tourist office at ⓐ Place Ste Cécile, Albi ⓣ (05) 63 49 48 98 ⓦ www.albi-tourisme.com ⓔ accueil@albitourisme.com. See also the town hall website ⓦ www.mairie-albi.fr

⬇ *Medieval Pont Vieux, crossing the river at Albi*

## Cathédrale Ste Cécile

This huge cathedral is built like a fortress, imposing itself over the surrounding city with its expanse of red brick and night-time illumination. Inside it is full of delicate Renaissance paintings, beautiful carved screens and huge stained glass windows. It is worth paying the small charge to see the frescoes. ⓐ Place Ste Cécile, Albi ⓔ ste-cecile@wanadoo.fr ⓒ 08.30–18.45, June–Sept; 09.00–12.00, 14.00–18.30, Oct–May. Admission charge for Grand Choeur

## Cordes-sur-Ciel

This medieval bastide is one of the prettiest villages in France, set high above the surrounding countryside – as the name suggests, it is floating in the clouds. Here they make a dry white, lightly sparkling Perlé wine, which takes its distinctive flavour from the surrounding limestone-soaked vineyards. Other medieval bastides, while you're in the area, include Castelnau-de-Montmiral, Puycelci and Penne

⬥ *Cordes-sur-Ciel in the Cerou valley*

## Domaine Le Roc

A friendly welcome is almost always extended at this family-run château, even during fraught times such as harvest. You should book during the week, but can just turn up at weekends during opening hours. ⓐ 61 route de Toulouse, Fronton ⓣ (05) 61 82 93 90 ⓦ www.leroc-fronton.com ⓔ infos@leroc-fronton.com ⓛ 10.00–12.00, 14.00–18.00

## Fronton

The Côtes de Frontonnais is seen as Toulouse's local wine. This area is also known as the orchard of France, so make sure you pick up lots of local fruit for picnics. Especially good are the chasselas grapes, and the ripe, fragrant peaches. Also worth seeking out is le Montauriol de Montauban, a delicious chocolate speciality from the nearby town of Montauban.

Information on sights, attractions and events in Fronton is available from the town hall. ⓐ 1 Espl Marcorelle, Fronton ⓣ (05) 62 79 92 92 ⓦ www.mairie-fronton.fr ⓔ mairie.fronton@wanadoo.fr

## Millau Viaduct

If you've got a head for heights, don't miss Sir Norman Foster's Millau Viaduct, crossing the Tarn River gorge in the Cevennes national park. This is slightly further away from Toulouse (at least a 2.5 hour drive) but is spectacular.

## Pont Vieux

An eyeglass bridge over the Tarn River that has been in existence since 1035. A perfect photo spot.

## CULTURE

### Albi grand prix racing

In September every year, Albi gives itself over to race fever. Contact the tourist office for information (see page 119 for contact details).

### Albi jazz and classical music festivals

June sees a popular jazz festival in Albi, with events all over the town. A classical music festival is held over the last two weeks of July. Contact the tourist office for information.

### Boat trips

You can take trips along the Tarn river in the flat-bottomed *gabare* boats that traditionally took the wine upriver to Bordeaux for distribution. ⓐ Chalet Albi Croisières (beneath the Palais de la Berbie), Albi ⓣ (05) 63 43 59 63 ⓦ www.albi-croisieres.com ⓔ safaraid@wanadoo.fr ⓛ Trips at 11.00, 11.45, 14.00–18.00, June–Sept. Admission charge

### Golf Albi-Lasbordes

An 18-hole golf course with a good restaurant and bar.
ⓐ Chemin Las Bordes, Albi ⓣ (05) 63 54 98 07 ⓦ www.golfalbi.com
ⓔ contact@golfalbi.com ⓛ 08.30–19.00. Admission charge

### Jardin des Paradis

A contemporary, Japanese-inspired garden in the middle of Cordes-sur-Ciel with a lovely mix of flowers, vegetation and quiet meditative corners. ⓐ Place du Théron, Cordes-sur-Ciel ⓣ (05) 63 56 29 77 ⓦ www.cordes-sur-ciel.org

🕐 14.00–18.00, Apr–June; 10.30–19.00, July & Aug; 14.00–18.00, Sept & Oct. Admission charge, under 8s free

## Musée des Beaux-Arts

Wide-ranging exhibits from contemporary sculptures to romantic painters. ⓐ Château de Foucard, Ave Dom Vayssette, Gaillac ① (05) 63 57 18 25 Ⓦ www.ville-gaillac.fr ⓔ patrimoine@ville-gaillac.fr 🕐 10.00–12.00, 14.00–18.00 Wed–Mon, Apr–Oct; 10.00–12.00, 14.00–18.00 Fri–Sun, Nov–Mar. Admission charge

## Rando'Jazz

October in Fronton sees a mix of walking and music with this unusual jazz festival. Most of the venues are within easy walking distance. Contact the town hall for more information (see page 121).

### GAILLAC WINE ROUTE AND FESTIVAL

The beautiful wine town of Gaillac has large cobbled squares, elegant bridges over the river Tarn, and a very attractive *Maison des Vins* set in the beautiful surroundings of the Château de Foucard. Throughout the summer, music and tastings are held in the courtyard every Friday evening. For one weekend in August, the *Maison* gives itself over to a festival of wine in celebration of the town's history of wine making, which dates back to the 1st century.
ⓐ Abbaye St Michel, Gaillac ① (05) 63 57 15 40
Ⓦ www.vins-gaillac.com ⓔ civg@vins-gaillac.com
🕐 10.00–12.00, 14.00–18.00 Mon–Sat

The town also has a well-organised and signed wine route full of welcoming characters. A few particularly good wine makers to visit are:

**Robert Plageoles** A local legend, with the complete library of traditional local grape varieties. He has rediscovered some that almost disappeared years ago. Ask for a sample of his wines made from grapes dried on straw mats. ⓐ Domaine des Tres Cantous, Cahuzac sur Vère ⓣ (05) 63 33 90 40 ⓔ robert-bernard.plageoles@wanadoo.fr ⓛ 08.00–12.00, 14.00–18.00 Mon–Fri

**Alain Rotier** A dynamic young wine maker who speaks great English and knows the area intimately. His Cuvée Renaissance gets consistent plaudits, and he's full of good suggestions for where to eat and drink. ⓐ Petit Nareye, Cadalen, Gaillac ⓣ (05) 63 41 75 14 ⓦ www.domaine-rotier.com ⓔ rotier@terre.net.fr ⓛ 08.00–12.00, 14.00–19.00 Mon–Sat Ⓐ A68 exit 10, follow signs direct to the Domaine

**Saveurs et Senteurs du Frontonnais (Food and Flavours of Fronton)**
A big festival is held in Fronton on the last weekend of August. There's jazz and blues to keep you entertained and local producers of everything from foie gras to honey. Contact the town hall for more information (see page 121 for contact details).

**Toulouse Lautrec Museum**
Lautrec was born in Albi and this museum contains over 500 examples of his work, from early pencil sketches right

up to his famous Paris brothel scenes. **ⓐ** Palais de la Berbie, Place Ste Cécile, Albi **ⓣ** (05) 63 49 48 70 **ⓦ** www.musee-toulouse-lautrec.com **ⓛ** 09.00–18.00, July & Aug; 10.00–12.00, 14.00–18.00, Sept–June. Admission charge

## TAKING A BREAK & AFTER DARK

*See also Accommodation section on page 126.*

**La Calèche £** Among the French bistro classics you'll find a few good vegetarian platters. **ⓐ** 6 rue de la Piale, Albi **ⓣ** (05) 63 54 15 52 **ⓛ** 12.00–14.00, 20.00–22.30

**Le Grand Pontié £** Large and airy, with brasserie downstairs, pizzeria upstairs, and pavement café outside. Good view overlooking the main square. **ⓐ** Place du Vigan, Albi **ⓣ** (05) 63 54 16 34 **ⓔ** cafelepontie@wanadoo.fr **ⓛ** 12.00–14.00, 19.00–23.30

**La Falaise ££** Lovely outside courtyard at this restaurant in the heart of the Gaillac wine routes, where you can eat beneath huge old trees. **ⓐ** Routes de Cordes, Cahuzac-sur-Vère **ⓣ** (05) 63 33 96 31 **ⓦ** www.lafalaiserestaurant.com **ⓔ** guillaume.salvan@wanadoo.fr **ⓛ** 12.00–14.00, 19.30–22.30 Tues–Sun

**Le Relais de la Vère ££** At the entrance to this pretty village you'll receive a friendly welcome and excellent varied menus. Music some evenings. **ⓐ** Anne Depelchin, Le Verdier **ⓣ** (05) 63 33 95 87 **ⓦ** www.lerelaisdelavere.com **ⓛ** 09.00–19.00 Mon–Wed, 09.00–18.00 Thurs, 15.00–19.00 Sat, 10.00–19.00 Sun

**L'Epicurien £££** Worth its reputation, this is a stylish restaurant with good quality ingredients and a small, focused menu. Fun ideas for children also, like special tasting menus. ⓐ 42 pl Jean Jaurès, Albi ⓣ (05) 63 53 10 70 ⓦ www.restaurantlepicurien.com ⓛ 12.00–14.00, 20.00–22.30; closed Aug

## ACCOMMODATION

**Camping Le Caussels £** Just a few miles outside of Millau, this very basic campsite makes a good base for exploring the region if you don't mind roughing it for a day or two. ⓐ Val de Caussels, Route de Millau, Albi ⓣ (05) 63 60 37 06 ⓛ Apr–Oct ⓝ Bus: 5 from Place du Vigan

**Hôtel George V £** Friendly hotel with good sized rooms, near to the bus and railway stations. ⓐ 27-29 av Maréchal Joffre, Albi ⓣ (05) 63 54 24 16 ⓦ www.hotelgeorgev.com

**Hôtel-Restaurant de Vieil Alby ££** Small, good value rooms at this very central hotel, but what really swings it here is the restaurant, where you can eat fantastic seasonal food. ⓐ 25 rue Henri de Toulouse Lautrec, Albi ⓣ (05) 63 54 14 69 ⓦ http://perso.orange.fr/le-vieil-alby ⓔ levieilalby@wanadoo.fr

**Le Grand Ecuyer ££–£££** A Michelin-starred chef in the kitchen makes this hotel especially inviting. ⓐ Haut de la Cité, Cordes-sur-Ciel ⓣ (05) 63 53 79 50 ⓦ www.legrandecuyer.fr ⓛ Mar–Oct

▶ *Le Pont Saint Pierre*

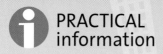

# Directory

## GETTING THERE

### By air

Toulouse Blagnac Airport (see page 50) is served by many UK and Irish airlines, including British Airways, BMI and Aer Lingus. The flight time from London is approximately 90 minutes.

**Air France** ☎ 08 20 82 08 20 Ⓦ www.airfrance.fr

**EasyJet** ☎ 08 25 08 25 08 Ⓦ www.easyjet.com

**Aer Lingus** ☎ 01 70 20 00 72 Ⓦ www.aerlingus.ie

**British Airways** ☎ 08 25 82 54 00 Ⓦ www.britishairways.com

**BMI** ☎ 01 41 91 87 04 Ⓦ www.flybmi.com

Many people are aware that air travel emits CO2, which contributes to climate change. You may be interested in the possibility of lessening the environmental impact of your flight through Climate Care, which offsets your CO2 emissions by funding environmental projects around the world. Visit Ⓦ www.climatecare.org

### By rail

To get from London to Toulouse by rail, take the Eurostar to Paris and then change to a TGV from Paris to Toulouse. The trip should take about 10 hours, and trains run regularly throughout the day. Return fares are often very good value.

**Eurostar** for cross-Channel trains ☎ (08705) 186 186 Ⓦ www.eurostar.com

**SNCF for trains within France** ☎ (08) 92 35 35 35 Ⓦ www.voyages-sncf.com

**Thomas Cook European Rail Timetable** ⓘ (01733) 416 477
ⓦ www.thomascookpublishing.com

### By road

The A62 motorway runs south from Bordeaux to Toulouse, carrying on south to Carcassonne and Montpellier. The journey from Bordeaux to Toulouse takes between two and three hours. The A1 goes from Paris to Toulouse, with drive time around eight hours. It is just about possible to drive from the UK to Toulouse, via Calais, in one day.

⬣ *The TGV brings Toulouse within easy reach of Paris*

Remember to bring both parts of your driving licence and to inform your insurance company before driving to France. You should carry a copy of your valid insurance certificate.

When you are in the region, information on traffic is available on ☎ (05) 61 12 77 77

Eurolines is Europe's largest coach operator, serving all of France. ⓦ www.eurolines.com

## ENTRY FORMALITIES

EU citizens can travel to France without a visa. For citizens of the USA, Canada, Australia, New Zealand and South Africa, visits of up to three months do not require a visa. Visitors from other countries do require a visa. All visitors need a passport.

EU citizens may bring into France personal possessions and goods for personal use, provided they have been bought in the EU. For full regulations visit ⓦ www.douane.gouv.fr

Animals entering France need a European (EU) Pet Passport. This is a booklet which contains all the relevant information about your pet, including an identification number and proof of a valid vaccine against the rabies virus. Animals travelling within any European Union countries other than Ireland, Sweden, Malta and the United Kingdom also need to have identification by microchip or tattoo. Tattoos are only acceptable until July 2011. All vets should have the relevant information and be able to get your animal ready for travelling with you.

## MONEY

The currency of France is the euro (€). 1 euro = 100 cents (also called eurocents). Euros come in notes of €5, €10, €20, €50, €100,

€200, €500. Coins are in denominations of €1 and €2, and in cents worth 1c, 2c, 5c, 10c, 20c and 50c. For current exchange rates, check www.travelex.com or www.oanda.com

ATM machines are plentiful in Toulouse and are the easiest way to withdraw money while in the city. Traveller's cheques and foreign money can be cashed at most banks, bureaux de change and some hotels. You will need your passport as identification. Major international credit cards are accepted in most large stores and restaurants and in ATM machines.

## Tipping

A 15 per cent service charge is usually included in the bill in French restaurants, although often not in cafés. It is customary to add another 2–3 per cent on top if the service has been good, or to round the bill up to the nearest euro. Taxi drivers expect ten per cent of the fare on top, and hairdressers around the same. When staying in hotels, it is usual to tip staff a few euros for carrying baggage to rooms.

## HEALTH, SAFETY & CRIME

Tap water is safe to drink, and many public parks have drinking fountains. *Eau Non Potable* means the water is not safe to drink. At almost all restaurants, you will be given a *pichet d'eau* (jug of tap water) when you sit down.

No inoculations are necessary for British citizens travelling to France. If you have any queries, ask your doctor before leaving, pick up the Department of Health leaflet T5 'Health Advice for Travellers' from a post office, or visit the travel advice section of Ⓦ www.dh.gov.uk.

It is always advisable to take a small first aid kit with you, and to keep it in the car if you are travelling around. If you take regular medication take enough for your holiday, and you should consider packing your regular headache remedy. If travelling in summer, remember to take sun cream.

As in any big city, be careful of valuables, watch for pickpockets and lock your car and belongings up securely. At night, avoid the areas around the central railway station and between rue Bayard and allées Jean Jaurès, as well as the Boulevards. Be aware that there are a number of homeless people and beggars in Toulouse.

## OPENING HOURS
**Banks** ⏱ 09.00–12.30, 14.00 or 14.30–16.30 or 17.00 Mon–Fri
**Shops** ⏱ 09.30/10.00–12.30 and 14.00–19.00 Mon–Sat
**Chemists** ⏱ 08.30 or 09.00–12.00 and 14.00–19.00 Mon–Sat
**Restaurants** ⏱ 12.00–14.00/14.30, 19.00–22.30 daily, although some restaurants are closed on Mondays.

## TOILETS
There are public toilets at several places in the centre of Toulouse and most are clean and well maintained. There are separate ones for men and women, and most will have an entrance fee. The airport and the railway station both have good public toilets, and most museums are also a good bet for clean facilities.

## CHILDREN
Toulouse is a very child-friendly city, and small children are welcomed in almost all hotels, cafés and restaurants. Pharmacies

sell nappies and baby food and all the other essentials. Remember in summer it can get very hot, so even when wandering around the city make sure your children are wearing protective clothing, sun cream and hats.

The city is full of attractions for children, not least the Cité de l'Espace with its IMAX cinema and Little Astronauts play area. Other good bets are:

**Centre Régional d'Information Jeunesse** Plenty of ideas on how to keep little ones entertained. ⓐ 17 rue de Metz ⓣ (05) 61 21 20 20 ⓦ www.crij.org ⓔ crij-tlse@crij.org ⓛ 10.00–18.00 Mon–Fri, 10.00–13.00, 14.00–17.00 Sat Ⓝ Metro: Capitole

**L'Envers du Décor** An interactive theatre show suitable for children from the age of seven. The name means 'behind the scenes' and children in the audience also help put on the show. ⓐ Théâtre Le Fil à Plomb, 30 rue de la Chaîne ⓣ (05) 62 30 99 77 ⓦ lefilaplomb.free.fr ⓔ lefilaplomb@free.fr Ⓝ Metro: Capitole

**Fondation Bemberg** A museum and gallery running several events for children, from brass plate rubbing to story-telling. ⓐ Hôtel d'Assézat, Place d'Assézat ⓣ (05) 61 12 06 89 ⓦ www.fondation-bemberg.fr ⓔ accueil@fondation-bemberg.fr ⓛ 10.00–12.30, 13.30–18.00 Tues–Fri Ⓝ Metro: Capitole. Admission charge

**PlayPark** A new playground with over 1000 sq m of play space, for children from 0 to 12. ⓐ 18 route de Muret, Portet-sur-Garonne ⓣ (05) 62 87 91 97 ⓦ www.playpark.fr ⓔ info@playpark.fr ⓛ 16.00–20.00 Tues, Thur & Fri, 10.00–21.00 Wed, Sat & Sun Ⓝ Car: N20 from Toulouse to Porter sur Garonne. Admission charge

## COMMUNICATIONS

### Internet

There are a number of internet cafés around the city, and increasingly hotels and some cafés have wireless zones with either free or paid-for access. The streets around Place du Capitole have a number of small internet cafés that are cheap and cheerful.

**Cyber King** @ 31 rue Gambetta ☏ (05) 62 27 13 97
🕐 10.30–22.00 Mon–Sat, 14.00–21.00 Sun Ⓝ Metro: Capitole

**Resomania** @ 85 rue Pargaminières ☏ (05) 62 30 25 64
🕐 09.30–00 Mon–Fri, 12.00–00.00 Sat & Sun Ⓝ Metro: Capitole

### Phone

Card-operated public phone boxes are available across Toulouse. You can buy a *télécarte* (phone card) at a *tabac* (newsagent). For Directory Enquires call ☏ 118 712 from any phone.

To call abroad from France, dial 00 for an international connection, then your own country code, then the area code

### TELEPHONING TOULOUSE

To call Toulouse from abroad, dial your own international prefix (00 in most countries) then 33 for France. The area code for southwest France, including Toulouse, is 05, followed by a number which is always eight digits in length. When dialling from abroad, drop the first 0, to leave 00 33 5 and the eight-digit number. When dialling Toulouse from anywhere in France, dial 05 and then the eight-digit number.

and phone number you desire leaving out the initial 'o'. Country code for the UK is 44, for the Republic of Ireland is 353, for USA or Canada is 1, for Australia is 61, for New Zealand is 64, and for South Africa is 27.

## Post

There are over 25 post offices throughout downtown Toulouse. Post offices sell telephone cards, and usually have photocopiers or a fax machine available for public use. Most post offices have coin-operated machines for buying stamps and weighing packages if you don't want to wait in line.

Post boxes are yellow and easy to spot. Stamps can be bought either from the post office or from a *tabac* (newsagents).

The main post office in Toulouse is very close to Place du Capitole. ⓐ 9 rue Lafayette ⓣ (05) 61 33 40 00 ⓦ www.laposte.fr ⓛ 08.00–19.00 Mon–Fri, 08.00–12.00 Sat ⓜ Metro Capitole

## ELECTRICITY

France runs on 220 volts with 2-pin plugs. British appliances will need an adaptor, easily obtained from any electrical or hardware store, or from the airport. US and other equipment designed for 110 volts will need a transformer.

## TRAVELLERS WITH DISABILITIES

Toulouse airport and railway stations have good access points for travellers who need extra assistance, and there are lifts in all the metro stations and most of the larger hotels. However, buses tend to be ill-equipped, and there are many hotels which do not have bathrooms and bedrooms that are easily adapted to wheelchairs. Useful organisations for information and advice include:

**RADAR** The principal UK forum and pressure group for people with disabilities. ⓐ 12 City Forum, 250 City Road, London EC1V 8AF ⓣ (020) 7250 3222 ⓕ (020) 7250 0212 ⓦ www.radar.org.uk ⓔ radar@radar.org.uk

**SATH (Society for Accessible Travel & Hospitality)** Advises US-based travellers with disabilities. ⓐ 347 Fifth Ave, Suite 605, New York 10016 ⓣ (212) 447 7284 ⓕ (212) 447 1928 ⓦ www.sath.org ⓔ sathtravel@aol.com

**Association des Paralysés en France Délégation Départementale des Alpes-Maritime**s ⓐ 21 blvd Mantéga Righi, 06100 Nice ⓣ (04) 92 15 78 70 ⓕ (04) 93 44 19 18 ⓦ www.apf.asso.fr ⓔ apf.dd06@wanadoo.fr

## TOURIST INFORMATION

To reach any tourist board in France, dial 3264 and clearly say the name of the town or city you are interested in. You will be put through automatically to the correct tourist office. Calls cost 34 cents per min.

**Maison de La France** (French Tourist Board) has a UK branch that can offer plenty of info before you leave. ⓐ 178 Piccadilly, W1J 9AL London ⓣ 09068 244 123 (calls cost 60p per min) ⓕ (020) 7493 6594 ⓦ www.franceguide.com ⓔ info.uk@franceguide.com

**Office de Tourisme de Toulouse** is the main tourist office in Toulouse. It is housed in a 16th century tower and former dungeon, making it something of an attraction in itself. ⓐ Square du Général Charles de Gaulle ⓣ (05) 61 11 02 22 ⓕ (05) 61 23 74 97 ⓦ www.toulouse-tourisme.com

ⓔ infos@ot-toulouse.fr 🕐 09.00–18.00 Mon–Fri, 09.00–12.30, 14.00–18.00 Sat, 10.00–12.30 14–17.00 Sun, Oct–May; 09.00–19.00 Mon–Sat, 10.30–17.15 Sun June–Sept Ⓜ Metro: Capitole

**Maison du Midi Pyrénées** (Comité Régional du Tourisme Midi-Pyrénées) ⓐ 54 blvd de l'Embouchure ☎ (05) 61 13 55 55 🅕 (05) 61 47 17 16 ⓦ www.tourisme-midi-pyrenees.com ⓔ maison-midi-pyrenees@crtmp.com Ⓜ Metro: Capitole

## BACKGROUND READING

*Le Petit Prince (The Little Prince)* by Antoine de Saint Exupéry. A classic. Any books by the same author can get you in the mood for a trip to Toulouse.

*Last Tango in Toulouse* by Mary Moody. Set in the countryside around Toulouse, this looks at what happens when a gardening writer gives it all up to start again in southwest France and embarks on an affair.

*Wines of Southwest France* by Paul Strang. A good overview of the treasures that can be found in the area.

# Emergencies

The following are emergency free-call numbers:

**Ambulance** ☎ 15
**Fire** ☎ 18
**Police** ☎ 17
All emergency services from a mobile phone ☎ 112

Note that in France, *pompiers* (firemen) also deal with first aid and most other emergency situations.

## MEDICAL SERVICES

Visitors from the UK require a European Health Insurance Card (EHIC), which guarantees emergency treatment.

**Emergency doctors**
**SOS Médecins (day)** ☎ (05) 61 33 00 00
**SOS Médecin de garde (night)** ☎ (05) 61 49 66 66 or (05) 61 22 00 00
See ⊛ www.sosmedecins-france.fr

**English-speaking dentists**
**Dr Nicole Garbasky** @ 45 allées Jean Jaurès ☎ (05) 61 62 30 58
**Dr Jean Michel** @ 135 route de Seilh, Aussonne ☎ (05) 61 85 14 19

**Hospitals**
**CHR Rangueil** @ Ave Jean Poulhes ☎ (05) 61 32 25 33
**CHR Purpan** @ Place du Docteur Baylac ☎ (05) 61 77 22 33
**Hôpital Larrey** @ 24 chemin de Pouvourville ☎ (05) 67 77 14 33
**Hôpital des Enfants (children's hospital)** @ 330 av de Grande Bretagne ☎ (05) 34 55 86 33

**After-hours pharmacy** 🅐 70–76 allées Jean Jaurès
🕿 (05) 61 62 38 05 🕘 20.00–08.00 Mon–Sat,
20.00–09.00 Sun and public holidays
**Centre Anti-Poisons (Poison Centre)** 🕿 (05) 61 49 33 33
**Urgence Vétérinaire (Emergency Vet)** 🕿 (05) 61 11 21 31

## POLICE
**Hôtel de Police (main police headquarters)**
🅐 23 blvd de l'Embouchure 🕿 (05) 61 12 77 77
**Lost Property** 🅐 17 place Intérieure St Cyprien 🕿 (05) 62 27 63 00

## EMBASSIES & CONSULATES
**Australia** 🅐 4 Rue Jean Rey, Paris 🕿 (01) 40 59 33 01
**Canada** 🅐 10 rue Jules de Rességuier, Toulouse 🕿 (05) 61 52 19 06
**Ireland** 🅐 4 rue Rude, Paris 🕿 (01) 44 17 67 67
**New Zealand** 🅐 7 ter, rue Leonard de Vinci, Paris 🕿 (01) 45 00 24 11
**South Africa** 🅐 59 Quai d'Orsay, Paris 🕿 (01) 53 59 23 23
**UK** 🅐 353 blvd Wilson, Bordeaux 🕿 (05) 57 22 21 10
**US** 🅐 25 allées Jean Jaurès, Toulouse 🕿 (05) 34 41 36 50

### EMERGENCY PHRASES

**Help!**   Au secours!   *Or secoors!*

**Call the police/fire service/ambulance!**
Appelez la police/les pompiers/un ambulance!
*Appeley la police/leh pompee-eh/un ambulance!*

### Send your thoughts to
# books@thomascook.com

- Found a great bar, club, shop or must-see sight that we don't feature?
- Like to tip us off about any information that needs a little updating?
- Want to tell us what you love about this handy little guidebook and more importantly how we can make it even handier?

Then here's your chance to tell all! Send us ideas, discoveries and recommendations today and then look out for your valuable input in the next edition of this title.

Email the above address (stating the title) or write to:
CitySpots Project Editor, Thomas Cook Publishing, PO Box 227, Coningsby Road, Peterborough PE3 8SB, UK.